Multimedia Systems and Applications

Series editor

Borko Furht, Florida Atlantic University, Boca Raton, USA

More information about this series at http://www.springer.com/series/6298

Ziyan Wu

Human Re-Identification

Springer

Ziyan Wu
Siemens Corporate Research
Princeton, NJ
USA

Multimedia Systems and Applications
ISBN 978-3-319-82235-8 ISBN 978-3-319-40991-7 (eBook)
DOI 10.1007/978-3-319-40991-7

Printed on acid-free paper

This Springer imprint is published by Springer Nature
The registered company is Springer International Publishing AG Switzerland

To my parents

Preface

This book covers all aspects of human re-identification problems related to computer vision and machine learning. Working from a practical perspective, it introduces novel algorithms and designs for human re-identification that bridge the gap between research and reality. The primary focus is on building a robust, reliable, distributed, and scalable smart surveillance system that can be deployed in real-world scenarios. The book also includes detailed discussions on pedestrian candidates' detection, discriminative feature extraction and selection, dimension reduction, distance/metric learning, and decision/ranking enhancement. In general the book is organized in three major parts:

First, we introduce the problem definition, challenges and current state of the art of intelligent video surveillance. In particular, we describe the scope of the human re-identification problem, and how it is related to similar computer vision problems such as image retrieval and cross-view object tracking. We also discuss how human re-identification techniques relate to general intelligent video surveillance and their possible extensions to non-surveillance problems.

Next, we discuss the general approaches in designing and planning the infrastructure for real-world human re-identification system. We start with single camera mathematical models and calibration approaches based on different calibration targets. Then we dig into the practical design and planning of a camera network, as well as its calibration approaches with or without overlapped field of view while ensuring reasonable measurement accuracy.

Last but not least, we address several important problems related to human re-identification in camera networks. Since surveillance cameras are typically mounted high above the ground plane, we introduce a sub-image rectification method to eliminate the effects of perspective distortion. Moreover, we propose a model for human appearance as a function of pose what can be used in extracting roughly viewpoint invariant features for the images of the target and the candidates. We demonstrate superior performance on human re-identification applications in a real-world scenario. We also proposed an efficient discriminative dimension reduction approach based on random projection and random forest metric learning to improve the training-time efficiency of metric learning algorithms. A method to hierarchically clustering image sequences while maximizing Fisher criterion is also designed specifically for multi-shot human re-identification problem removing the bias induced from unbalance samples in the training data.

Princeton, NJ, USA
February 2016

Ziyan Wu

Acknowledgments

First of all I would like to express my gratitude to my Ph.D. adviser, Dr. Richard J. Radke, for his inspiring guidance and continuous support. I have been greatly influenced by him during the past 5 years, not only for his scrupulous attitude and creative mind in doing research, but also for his wise opinions and philosophy in solving problems and cultivating abilities. He enlightened me with erudite knowledge in computer vision, and the invaluable skills he taught me in writing and presenting ideas will benefit me greatly in my future endeavors. I really appreciate his genuine care and providing such great opportunities for my study, research, and life. He is much more than an adviser to me.

I would like to thank many friends from Rensselaer Polytechnic Institute. We had been working on this challenging human re-identification project together and they contributed a lot to the work in this book. In particular I would like to thank Yang Li and Srikrishna Karanam, who helped me in solving many of the "impossible problems". It was always so enjoyable and inspiring to have technical and nontechnical discussions with you. This work would not have been possible without your inspiration and constructive suggestions.

I would also like to thank my colleagues at the Department of Homeland Security Center of Excellence, Awareness and localization of Explosive-Related Threats, and Siemens Corporate Research, for their help and support. Thanks to Edward Hertelendy and Michael Young from TSA, I can have the permission to work and collect data at the airport.

I am thankful to the Springer editors, Susan Lagerstrom-Fife and Jennifer Malat, for their enthusiasm, support, patience, and understanding while I am working on the book.

Last but not least, I would like to thank my family. I owe my deepest thanks to my parents, Jinlang and Xiaoya, for their perseverance in supporting me in every aspect. You are always my inexhaustible source of strength. To my wife Meng—thanks to all your devotion and sacrifices that I always managed to concentrate on my research. To my daughter, Julia, thanks for joining us and bringing us unlimited joy and happiness.

Part of the content in this book is based upon work supported by the U.S. Department of Homeland Security under Award Number 2008-ST-061-ED0001. The views and conclusions contained in this document are those of the authors and should not be interpreted as necessarily representing the official policies, either expressed or implied of the U.S. Department of Homeland Security.

Contents

Acronyms

BRIEF	Binary Robust Independent Elementary Features
BRISK	Binary Robust Invariant Scalable Keypoints
CMC	Cumulative Matching Characteristic
DF	Discriminative Features
DoG	Difference-of-Gaussian
FAST	Features from Accelerated Segment Test
FOV	Field of View
FREAK	Fast Retina Keypoint
ITML	Information Theoretic Metric Learning
KLT	Kanade–Lucas–Tomasi corner detector
LDML	Logistic Discriminant Metric Learning
LFDA	Local Fisher Discriminant Analysis
LMNN	Large Margin Nearest Neighbor
LPP	Locality Preserving Projections
PCCA	Pairwise Constrained Component Analysis
PP	Pose Prior
RAC	Radial Alignment Constraint
RDC	Relative Distance Comparison
SIFT	Scale-Invariant Feature Transform
SURF	Speeded Up Robust Features
SVM	Support Vector Machine

Part I
Video Surveillance and Human Re-identification

Intelligent video surveillance is one of the most essential application domains of computer vision and machine learning technologies, and human re-identification is one of the most challenging problems in intelligent video surveillance. In the first part of this book, we are going to introduce the background and the current state of human re-identification.

Chapter 1
The Problem of Human Re-Identification

One of the ultimate goal of computer science is to endow computers in addition to exceptional speed of calculation with advanced intelligence, rich emotions, and accurate perceptions, just like those of humans. One major step toward that is to enable computers to sense like a human being. In particular, computer vision is the set of technologies that can make computers to see.

1.1 Surveillance and Computer Vision

Applications based on computer vision technologies are everywhere in our daily life. Social network platforms are tagging and classifying human faces on pictures user uploaded. Cellphone camera applications can easily guide you on obtaining a 360-degree panorama image. One can even unlock a computer without keying in pass code—by either using fingerprint scanner or even scanning his/her face in front of the web camera. 3D maps on your computer are reconstructed with a bunch of cameras and vision algorithms.

We are enjoying fun and conveniences brought by these applications. In fact, computer vision techniques are playing far more crucial roles in our lives. Factories are inspecting products and instruments with accurate and nondestructive vision inspection approaches; The future of self-driving cars are relying on vision perception methods; Clinical physician can conduct more efficient and effective operations with the help of automatic image-based device tracking and organ segmentation algorithms.

One other domain in which vision technologies are being developed is security surveillance such as target recognition, threat monitoring as well as criminal activity investigation. As a matter of fact, even nowadays most surveillance systems in mass transit environments including bus and train stations, and airports are still monitored by human operators. These environments are facing great challenges in protecting passengers from security threats and breaches. Even though increasingly advanced video surveillance systems have been deployed in tens of thousands of airports around

Z. Wu, *Human Re-Identification*, Multimedia Systems and Applications,
DOI 10.1007/978-3-319-40991-7_1

the world with analog video cameras being replaced by digital cameras gradually, and video tapes being replaced by advanced compact digital recording systems, the final link of the system responsible for triggering the alarms are still human officers. Just imagine these staff members watching hundreds of video monitors for at least eight hours continuously everyday. Previous research [1] has shown that the attention of most human individuals is likely to stray far below acceptable levels over such long time spans.

US Department of Homeland Security is spending billions of dollars for government agencies and public facilities to install advanced video surveillance systems, including the development of intelligent video analytic technologies, which can relieve human operators in surveillance tasks. With the rapid development of computer vision and artificial intelligence, many of the surveillance task can already be accomplished by computer programs, such as pedestrian detection, change detection, and flow tracking. However these tasks are all on relatively lower level, meaning decisions on whether or not triggering the alarms cannot be directly obtained with the output from these components. Although researchers have been looking at solving the higher level surveillance problems, e.g., multiple object tracking, target identities association, most of these algorithms are not ready to be deployed in real-world scenarios due to insufficient reliability, unable to adapt to change in environments and lack of computation scalability. One typical example among them is human re-identification problem [2], which is often considered as the most challenging surveillance problem for not just machines, but sometimes also for human.

1.2 Human Re-Identification

Recognizing the same human as he or she moves through a network of cameras with nonoverlapping fields of view is an important and challenging problem in security and surveillance applications. This is often called the re-identification or "re-id" problem. For example, in an airport security surveillance system, once a target has been identified in one camera by a user or program, we want to learn the appearance of the target and recognize him/her when he/she is observed by the other cameras. We call this type of re-id problem "tag-and-track". Human re-identification across cameras with nonoverlapping fields of view is one of the most important and difficult problems in video surveillance and analysis. The general process of human re-identification is shown in Fig. 1.1.

Once a target is tagged in a camera view, sub-image (shown as a red-bounding box in Fig. 1.1) will be extracted from the raw video frame to eliminate the background and clutters. Visual features will be extracted from the sub-image to form the "signature" of the target, which will be used to match with the signatures from all candidates from other camera views after the target left the view where he/she was tagged initially. Finally the candidates with the highest matching score will be considered as the top candidate of the target. In reality, additional reasoning will be taken into account in the decision stage, including spatial and temporal constraints and priors.

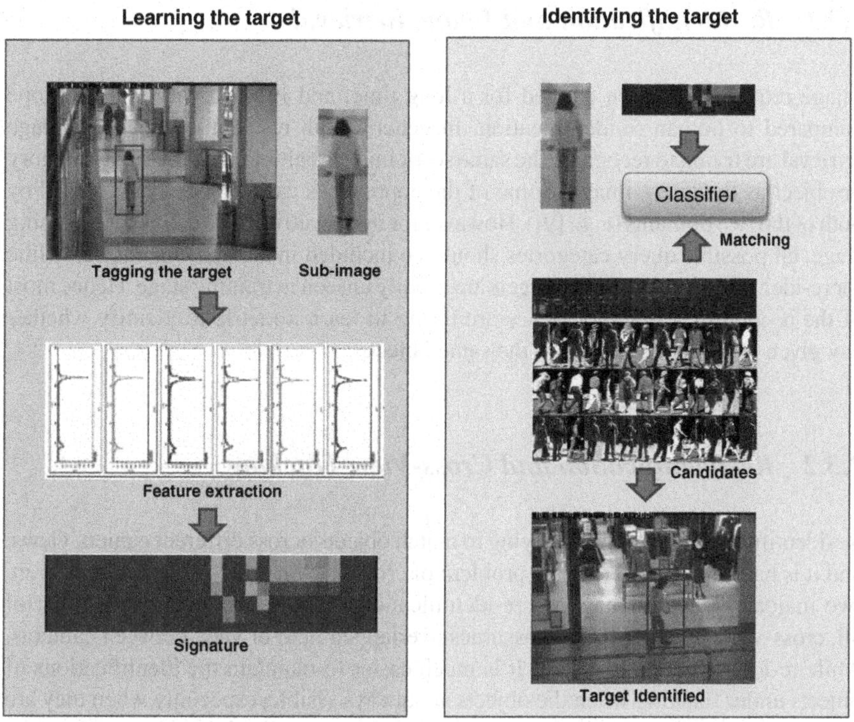

Fig. 1.1 Process of human re-identification

1.3 Looking at People

Traditional biometric methods such as face [3], gait [4], or silhouette [5] recognition have been widely used in human identity recognition; however they are difficult to apply to the re-id problem since most surveillance cameras' resolution is too poor to get a clear image of the target. This is quite different from the case of person identification with high-definition videos [6–8], where more sophisticated and complex features can be extracted. Unfortunately in real-world scenarios, high-definition videos are usually not available.

That is the reason why we have to look at people differently, which is also the reason why human re-identification problem is so challenging. Researchers were trying to reconsider this problem by observing the human vision system. When a target is far away, one tends to identify it by extracting high-level attributes, from style and color of hair, to color of cloths and belongings. Given a moving target, people would also pay attention to the way he/she moves. These observations became the essence of the way for computer algorithms to look at human objects in human re-identification applications.

1.3.1 Re-Identification and Image Retrieval

Image retrieval has been studied for a long time, and it has a very similar scope compared to human re-identification. In general both re-identification and image retrieval are trying to recognize the same set of images belonging to the same category or object as the query image. Some of the approaches can potentially be shared by both of the two domains (e.g., [9]). However for image retrieval, usually in the training stage, all possible query categories should be included in the training dataset, while for re-identification, the probe targets are usually unseen in training stage. Hence most of the re-identification approaches are trying to learn a metric to identify whether any given image pairs belong to the same object.

1.3.2 Re-Identification and Cross-View Tracking

Re-identification is essentially trying to match objects across different camera views, and it is natural to relate it to the problem of cross-view tracking. However there are two major distinctions between re-identification and cross-view tracking. First of all, cross-view tracking usually assumes overlapped field of view between cameras, while re-identification does not. It is much easier to maintain the identifications of objects under tracking when the objects are always visible, especially when they are in transit from one camera view to another, where usually they are suppose to be seen by both of the two views at least briefly. Second, cross-view tracking heavily relies on temporal information while usually no temporal information is available for re-identification, since in real-world scenarios, visual coverage of the environment is very limited and it is usually unpredictable when the target is going to show up in another view of camera. Last but not least, since very few prior can be used to determine which camera view is the target that is going to show up next, candidates from many (sometimes all) camera views need to be match with the target, while only candidates in the current view need to be matched, even for some tracking-by-detection methods (e.g., [10]).

1.3.3 Real-World Applications

So far there are only several notable real-world applications of human re-identification. Among them, there are only few real-time systems. In [11] we have presented an end-to-end human re-identification system deployed at a mid-size US airport. The system consists of a camera network with approximately 10 network cameras looking at the exits of a terminal. Figure 1.2 shows the floor plan of one of its subsystems. As it can be seen that some of the cameras share partially overlapped field of view while some do not.

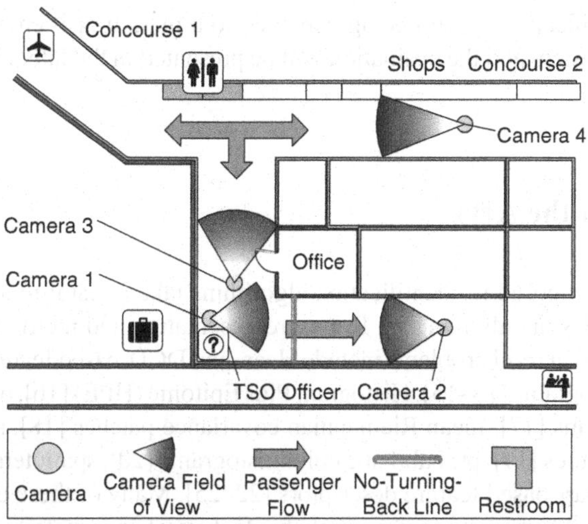

Fig. 1.2 Floor plan of a real-time human re-identification system deployed in an airport

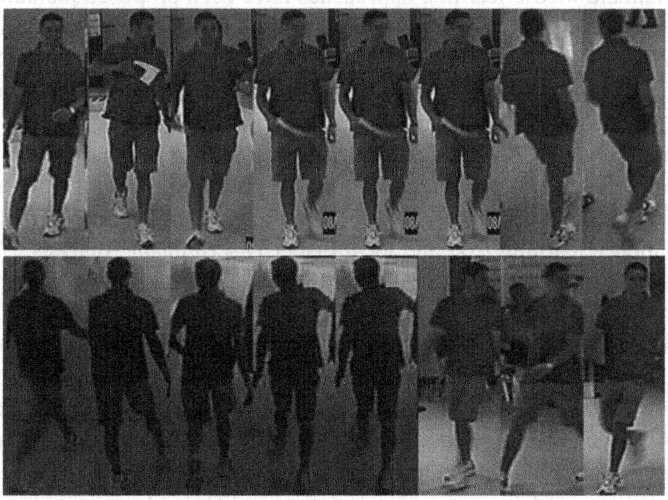

Fig. 1.3 An example sequence from multiple cameras of a passenger going through the exit

A sample sequence of a passenger going through the exit captured by the camera network is shown in Fig. 1.3. It can be seen that the illumination change is quite obvious, making the re-identification task rather difficult.

The system has been running for almost two years at the airport continuously and has reported over 90 % of rank-5 detection rate. After extensive testing and evaluation, the system has proven to be robust and reliable, and this is by far the first working human re-identification system being deployed to a mass transit environment. The details of this system and the evaluation will be presented in the later chapters of this book.

1.4 State of the Arts

Most recently proposed re-identification algorithms take a feature-based approach. These approaches mainly focus on feature representation and metric learning. Feature models used in re-id problems include Haar- and DCD-based features [12], color and texture histograms [13–15], Histogram Plus Epitome (HPE) [16], quantized local feature histograms [17], mean Riemannian covariance patches [18], symmetry and asymmetry features [19], probabilistic color histograms [20], spatiotemporal appearance [21] and part-based feature descriptors [22–25]. Many of these descriptors are high-dimensional and contain some unreliable features; hence metric model learning and feature selection are also critical problems for re-id.

Many standard metric learning approaches have been proposed including Large Margin Nearest Neighbor (LMNN) [26], Information Theoretic Metric Learning (ITML) [27], Logistic Discriminant Metric Learning (LDML) [3], LMNN with option of rejection (LMNN-R) [28], impostor-based LMNN [29], relative distance comparison (RDC) [30], RankSVM [15], boosting [13, 31], Mahalanobis distance metric [32], PCCA [33] and covariance metric [34]. Other metric learning approaches include online feature selection [8], set-based methods [14], attribute-sensitive feature importance learning [35], dissimilarity profile analysis [36], unsupervised salience learning [37] and local Fisher Discriminant Analysis [38]. Most of these are general metric learning algorithms from machine learning applied to the re-identification problem, among which RDC [30] and RankSVM [15] are most popular, and are extensively evaluated on most standard datasets. We selected these two methods to evaluate the performance improvement of our proposed algorithms.

Based on the above-featured model and metric learning approaches, additional techniques have also been introduced to improve the performance of re-id, including taking into account the spatial-temporal information of camera networks [21, 23, 39, 40], descriptive and discriminative classification [31], and panoramic appearance models [41].

1.5 Beyond Security Monitoring

The techniques developed for human re-identification will not be only beneficial to security surveillance. Core analytic such as metric learning and feature extraction can be easily applied to other domains such as access control, object recognition, image search, and traffic monitoring. Take traffic monitoring as an example, the image quality of cameras mounted on highways are similar to those you can find in airports. Hence the way we look at people in human re-identification applications can also be used to look at vehicles. In fact, the way that signatures extracted for targets in human re-identification has proven to be more reliable and generally applicable to all kinds of recognition tasks, which is a core component for autonomous perception systems such as robots and self-driving car.

1.6 Discussion

In this chapter, we introduce the concept of video surveillance, and the challenges it is facing. In particular, we discussed the definition, state-of-the-art approaches, as well as applications of the human re-identification problem. At the end we look beyond and proposed the possibilities of extending the techniques of human re-identification to other non-security-surveillance-related domains.

References

1. M.W. Green, The appropriate and effective use of security technologies in U.S. schools. Sandia National Laboratories, Albuquerque, NM, Tech. Rep. NCJ 178265, 1999
2. R. Vezzani, D. Baltieri, R. Cucchiara, People reidentification in surveillance and forensics: a survey. ACM Comput. Surv. **46**(2), 29.1–29.37 (2013)
3. M. Guillaumin, J. Verbeek, C. Schmid, Is that you? Metric learning approaches for face identification, in *IEEE International Conference on Computer Vision*, Kyoto, Japan, 2009
4. L. Wang, T. Tan, H. Ning, W. Hu, Silhouette analysis-based gait recognition for human identification. IEEE Trans. Pattern Anal. Mach. Intell. **25**, 1505–1518 (2003)
5. D.N. Truong Cong, L. Khoudour, C. Achard, C. Meurie, O. Lezoray, People re-identification by spectral classification of silhouettes. Signal Process. **90** 2362–2374 (2010)
6. M. Tapaswi, Knock! Knock! Who is it? Probabilistic person identification in TV-series. in *IEEE Conference on Computer Vision and Pattern Recognition*, Newport, RI, 2012
7. K. Jungling, M. Arens, View-invariant person re-identification with an Implicit shape model, in *IEEE International Conference on Advanced Video and Signal-Based Surveillance*, Klagenfurt, Austria, 2011
8. M. Eisenbach, A. Kolarow, K. Schenk, K. Debes, H.-M. Gross, View invariant appearance-based person reidentification using fast online feature selection and score level fusion, in *IEEE International Conference on Advanced Video and Signal-Based Surveillance*, Beijing, China, 2012
9. L. Zheng et al., Query-adaptive late fusion for image search and person re-identification. in *IEEE International Conference on Computer Vision Pattern Recognition*, Boston, MA, 2015
10. A. Geiger, et al., 3D Traffic scene understanding from movable platforms. IEEE Trans. Pattern Anal. Mach. Intell. **36** 1012–1025 (2014)
11. O. Camps, et al., From the lab to the real world: re-identification in an airport camera network. in *IEEE Transactions on Circuits and Systems for Video Technology* (2016), pp. 1–1
12. S. Bk, E. Corvee, F. Bremond, M. Thonnat, Person Re-identification using Haar-based and DCD-based signature. in *IEEE International Conference on Advanced Video and Signal-Based Surveillance*, Boston, MA, 2010
13. D. Gray, Viewpoint invariant pedestrian recognition with an ensemble of localized features, in *European Conference on Computer Vision 2008*, Marseille, France, 2008

14. W. Zheng, S. Gong, T. Xiang, Transfer re-identification: from person to set-based verification, in *IEEE Conference on Computer Vision and Pattern Recognition '12*, Providence, RI, 2012
15. B. Prosser, W.-S. Zheng, S. Gong, T. Xiang, Person re-identification by support vector ranking. in *British Machine Vision Conference*, Aberystwyth, UK, 2010
16. L. Bazzani, M. Cristani, A. Perina, V. Murino, Multiple-shot person re-identification by chromatic and epitomic analyses. Pattern Recognit. Lett. **33**, 898–903 (2012)
17. L.F. Teixeira, L. Corte-Real, Video object matching across multiple independent views using local descriptors and adaptive learning. Pattern Recognit. Lett. **30**, 157–167 (2009)
18. S. Bak, E. Corvée, F. Brémond, M. Thonnat, Boosted human re-identification using Riemannian manifolds. Imag. Vis. Comput. **30**, 443–452 (2011)
19. M. Farenzena, L. Bazzani, A. Perina, Person re-identification by symmetry-driven accumulation of local features. in *IEEE Conference on Computer Vision and Pattern Recognition*, San Francisco, CA, 2010
20. A. D'Angelo, J.-L. Dugelay, People re-identification in camera networks based on probabilistic color histograms, in *IS&T/SPIE Electronic Imaging*, San Francisco, CA, 2011
21. N. Gheissari, T. Sebastian, Person reidentification using spatiotemporal appearance, in *IEEE Conference on Computer Vision and Pattern Recognition*, New York, NY, 2006
22. D.S. Cheng, M. Cristani, M. Stoppa, L. Bazzani, V. Murino, Custom pictorial structures for re-identification. in *British Machine Vision Conference*, Dundee, UK, 2011
23. R. Mazzon, S.F. Tahir, A. Cavallaro, Person re-identification in crowd. Pattern Recognit. Lett. **33**, 1828–1837 (2012)
24. S. Bak, E. Corvee, F. Bremond, M. Thonnat, Person Re-identification Using Spatial Covariance Regions of Human Body Parts. in *IEEE International Conference on Advanced Video and Signal-Based Surveillance*, Boston, MA, 2010
25. L. Bourdev, S. Maji, J. Malik, Describing people: a poselet-based approach to attribute classification. in *IEEE International Conference on Computer Vision*, Barcelona, Spain, 2011
26. K.Q. Weinberger, L.K. Saul, Distance metric learning for large margin nearest neighbor classification. J. Mach. Learn. Res. **10**, 207–244 (2009)
27. J.V. Davis, B. Kulis, P. Jain, S. Sra, I.S. Dhillon, Information-theoretic metric learning. in *International Conference on Machine Learning*, Corvallis, OR, 2007
28. M. Dikmen, E. Akbas, T. S. Huang, N. Ahuja, Pedestrian recognition with a learned metric. in *Asian Conferene on Computer Vision*, Queenstown, New Zealand, 2010
29. M. Hirzer, P.M. Roth, H. Bischof, Person re-identification by efficient impostor-based metric learning. in *IEEE International Conference on Advanced Video and Signal-Based Surveillance*, Beijing, China, 2012
30. W. Zheng, S. Gong, T. Xiang, Re-identification by Relative Distance Comparison. IEEE Trans. Pattern Anal. Mach. Intell. **35**, 653–668 (2012)
31. M. Hirzer, C. Beleznai, P. M. Roth, H. Bischof, Person re-identification by descriptive and discriminative classification," in *Scandinavian Conf. on Image Analysis*, Ystad Saltsjobad, Sweden, 2011
32. M. Hirzer, P. M. Roth, M. Köstinger, H. Bischof, Relaxed pairwise learned metric for person re-identification. in *European Conference. on Computer Vision 2012*, Florence, Italy, 2012
33. A. Mignon, F. Jurie, PCCA: a new approach for distance learning from sparse pairwise constraints. in *IEEE Conference on Computer Vision and Pattern Recognition*, Providence, RI, 2012
34. B. Slawomir, G. Charpiat, E. Corvée, F. Brémond, M. Thonnat, Learning to match appearances by correlations in a covariance metric space. in *European Conference on Computer Vision*, Florence, Italy, 2012
35. C. Liu, S. Gong, C. Loy, X. Lin, Person re-identification: what features are important? in *1st International Workshop on Re-Identification*, Florence, Italy, 2012
36. Z. Lin, L.S. Davis, Learning pairwise dissimilarity profiles for appearance recognition in visual surveillance. in *International Symposium on Visual Computing*, Las Vegas, Nevada, 2008
37. R. Zhao, W. Ouyang, X. Wang, Unsupervised salience learning for person re-identification. in *IEEE Conference on Computer Vision and Pattern Recognition*, Portland, OR, 2013

38. S. Pedagadi, J. Orwell, S. Velastin, Local fisher discriminant analysis for pedestrian re-identification. in *IEEE Conference on Computer Vision and Pattern Recognition*, Portland, OR, 2013
39. G. Lian, J. Lai, W.-S. Zheng, Spatial temporal consistent labeling of tracked pedestrians across non-overlapping camera views. Pattern Recognit. **44**, 1121–1136 (2011)
40. O. Javed, K. Shafique, Z. Rasheed, M. Shah, Modeling inter-camera space-time and appearance relationships for tracking across non-overlapping views. Comput. Vis. Imag. Underst. **109**, 146–162 (2008)
41. T. Gandhi, M.M. Trivedi, Person tracking and reidentification: introducing panoramic appearance map (PAM) for feature representation. Mach. Vis. Appl. **18**, 207–220 (2007)

Chapter 2
Features and Signatures

In this chapter, we will discuss a important aspect in the core analytic of human re-identification, that is, converting a raw image into identifiable and reliable features.

2.1 Feature Detection

Extracting representative features from objects is a useful way to detect and track targets. A feature is considered to be representative if it has expressive texture in a particular region. Also, a desirable feature should be invariant to changes in illumination and viewpoint.

Harris and Stephens [1] proposed a corner detector known as the Harris corner detector. Let $I(x, y)$ be the intensity of pixel (x, y) in a gray scale image $\mathbf{I}$ and $s(u, v)$ be the weighted sum of squared differences obtained by a shift (u, v) of the patch. We have

$$s(u, v) = \sum_{(x,y)} w(x, y) \left(I(x + u, y + v) - I(x, y)\right)^2 \tag{2.1}$$

in which

$$w(x, y) = \begin{cases} 1 & (x, y) \text{ is in the shifting patch} \\ 0 & \text{otherwise.} \end{cases} \tag{2.2}$$

Expanding $I(x + u, y + v)$ in a Taylor series around $(u, v) = 0$, we have

$$I(x + u, y + v) \approx I(x, y) + \frac{\partial I(x, y)}{\partial x} u + \frac{\partial I(x, y)}{\partial y} v. \tag{2.3}$$

Then Eq. (2.1) becomes

Z. Wu, *Human Re-Identification*, Multimedia Systems and Applications,
DOI 10.1007/978-3-319-40991-7_2

$$s(u,v) \approx \sum_{(x,y)} w(x,y)\left(I(x,y) + \frac{\partial I(x,y)}{\partial x}u + \frac{\partial I(x,y)}{\partial y}v - I(x,y)\right)^2 \tag{2.4}$$

$$= [x\ y]\,\mathbf{H}\,[x\ y]^{\top} \tag{2.5}$$

in which **H** is the Harris matrix denoted by

$$\mathbf{H} = \begin{bmatrix} \sum_{(x,y)} w(x,y)\left(\frac{\partial I(x,y)}{\partial x}\right)^2 & \sum_{(x,y)} w(x,y)\frac{\partial I(x,y)}{\partial x}\frac{\partial I(x,y)}{\partial y} \\ \sum_{(x,y)} w(x,y)\frac{\partial I(x,y)}{\partial x}\frac{\partial I(x,y)}{\partial y} & \sum_{(x,y)} w(x,y)\left(\frac{\partial I(x,y)}{\partial y}\right)^2 \end{bmatrix} \tag{2.6}$$

where the partial derivatives can be estimated by applying Gaussian derivative filter to the image. A response function for the corner is given by

$$R = \det(\mathbf{H}) - k \cdot \text{trace}(\mathbf{H})^2 \tag{2.7}$$

in which k is a tunable sensitivity factor (usually between 0.04 and 0.15). The detector is more sensitive when k is smaller. R is large positive value if both of the two eigenvalues are large. A Harris corner is found if the response of a patch is locally maximum and higher than a preset threshold.

Noble [2] introduced an alternative response measurement function amounting to a harmonic mean of eigenvalues from **H** as

$$R_n = \frac{2\det(\mathbf{H})}{\text{trace}(\mathbf{H}) + \varepsilon} \tag{2.8}$$

in which ε is an arbitrary very small positive constant in order to avoid dividing by zero.

Shi and Tomasi and Kanade [3, 4] improved this corner detector, known as the Kanade–Lucas–Tomasi (KLT) corner detector, so that the corners are more suitable for tracking. The KLT corner detector uses the criterion

$$\min(\lambda_1, \lambda_2) > T \tag{2.9}$$

in which (λ_1, λ_2) are the two eigenvalues of **H**, and T is a threshold. This way the corner detected by the KLT corner detector will be more reliable to be tracked over time.

Harris and KLT corner detectors are effective, but may be computationally intensive due to numerous multi-scale/Gaussian convolutions or eigenvalue computations, which make them unsuitable for real-time high-resolution video sequence processing.

Rosten and Drummond [5] proposed an algorithm called Features from Accelerated Segment Test, known as the FAST corner detector. Each candidate pixel is compared to a circle of surrounding pixels. The pixel is considered to be a feature if all the surrounding pixels on a contiguous arc of n pixels on the circle are much lighter or darker than the center pixel. The circle consists of 16 pixels and n is set to 12. Later, Rosten and Drummond [6, 7] improved the algorithm with machine learning algorithms, claiming great improvement in both performance and speed of the feature detector. With the improved FAST corner detector, as few as three intensity comparisons need to be performed to identify whether the candidate pixel is a FAST corner.

2.2 Descriptors

However, neither of these features is scale invariant. In order to compare distinctive features, feature descriptors need to be extracted from detected feature locations. Lowe [8] proposed the Scale-Invariant Feature Transform (SIFT) which has became very popular in many computer vision applications. First, the difference-of-Gaussian function (DoG) is used to detect potential interest points, defined as:

$$D(x, y, \sigma) = (G(x, y, k\sigma) - G(x, y, \sigma)) * I(x, y) = L(x, y, k\sigma) - L(x, y, \sigma) \tag{2.10}$$

in which $I(x, y)$ is the image to be processed and $G(x, y, \sigma)$ is a variable-scale Gaussian. $L(x, y, \sigma)$ is the space scale defined by the convolution of $G(x, y, \sigma)$ with $I(x, y)$. The DoG is a close approximation to the scale-normalized Laplacian of Gaussian proposed by Lindeberg [9].

Next, by eliminating edge responses and rejecting points with low contrast, keypoints are precisely localized. The orientation is assigned by analyzing the histogram of the gradient orientations of pixels in the neighbor region around the keypoint. A 128-dimensional descriptor is formed for each detected feature. Figures 2.1 and 2.2 show an example of an image mosaic from two views of a scene based on SIFT feature extraction.

2.3 Invariant Features

While SIFT is very effective for matching, its computation is time consuming, which prevents it from becoming popular in real-time applications. Bay et al. [10] improved this algorithm and proposed the Speeded Up Robust Features (SURF) detector. Instead of using multi-scale pyramids and applying convolution to each layer of increasing σ in SIFT, SURF uses a stack, which can be filtered by box filters approximating second-order Gaussian partial derivatives. With the help of integral images,

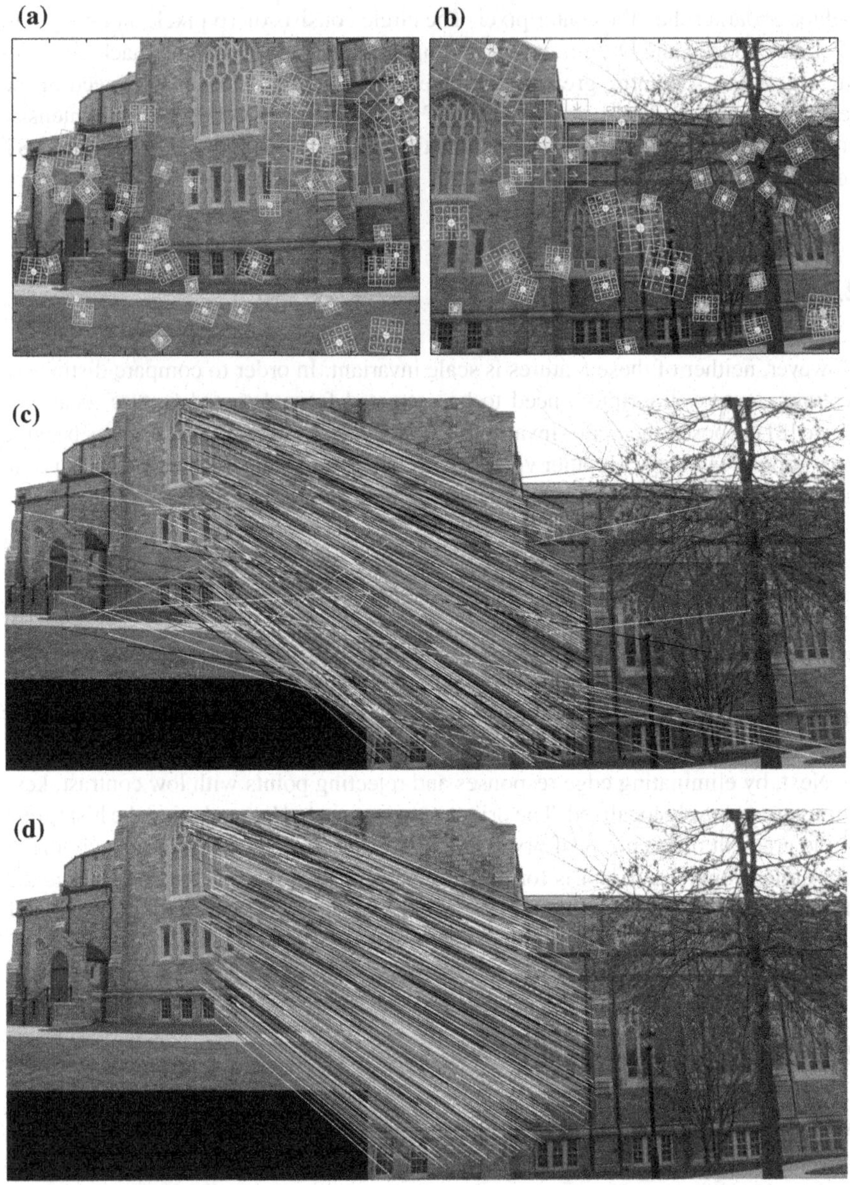

Fig. 2.1 SIFT features extracted from two views of the same scene. **a** Image A and its SIFT features. **b** Image B and its SIFT features. **c** 1279 matches found from the two views. **d** 1083 inlying matches found after RANSAC

Fig. 2.2 Image *mosaic* based on SIFT feature matching

rectangular box filters can be computed in real-time (e.g., ~25 fps on a VGA video stream), resulting in up to three times faster detection and matching with SURF compared to SIFT [11].

However, as mobile computing becomes more and more popular, even faster and lightweight algorithms for feature detection are needed. Calonder et al. [12] proposed a binary feature descriptor to replace the computation of Euclidean distance with Hamming distance, named Binary Robust Independent Elementary Features (BRIEF), which has a lighter computation load with similar performance as SIFT (though it is not rotation invariant). Based on the FAST corner detector and BRIEF descriptor, Ryvkee et al. [13] proposed Oriented Fast and Rotated BRIEF (ORB) maintaining fast computation while enabling rotation invariance. Leutenegger et al. [14] introduced Binary Robust Invariant Scalable Keypoints (BRISK) which are invariant to both scale and rotation, and are approximately 80 times faster in description and 30 times faster in matching compared to SIFT.

Recently, Alahi and Ortiz [15] proposed Fast Retina Keypoint (FREAK) inspired by the human visual system. A retinal sampling grid is used, which has higher point density near the center. The descriptor is constructed in a coarse-to-fine structure to enhance the performance of matching, resulting in 80 % faster performance on description and 30 % faster performance on matching compared to BRISK.

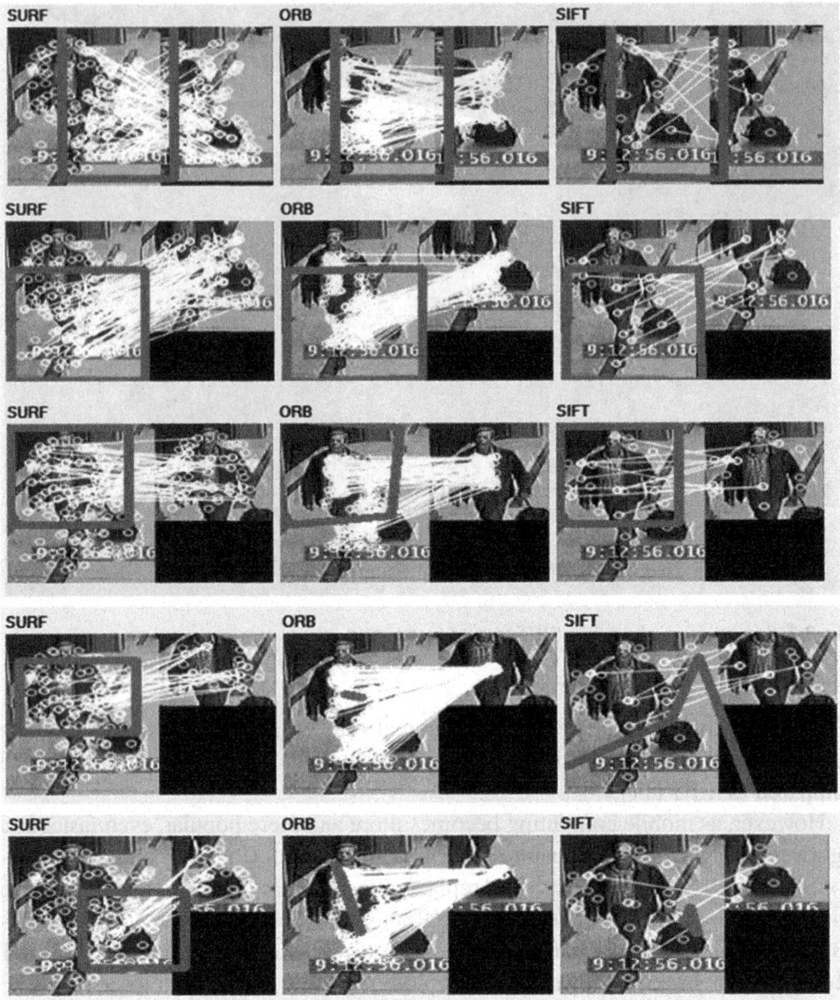

Fig. 2.3 Comparison of matching for SURF, ORB, and SIFT. *White lines* show the matches found, and *red rectangles* show the back-projected bounding box of the sub-image after RANSAC

Though SIFT and SURF are slower than these accelerated feature descriptors, they usually have better performance, especially with low-resolution images and complex lighting conditions. We conducted an experiment to compare the matching performance of SIFT, SURF, and ORB. A low-resolution image of a pedestrian captured by a surveillance camera is matched with five different sub-images of itself. The results are shown in Fig. 2.3. It can be seen that SURF has the best performance on matching accuracy. Though ORB is the fastest, it does not work well with low-resolution images.

2.4 Signatures in Human Re-Identification

Our approach to feature and descriptor extraction for a given image is similar to Gray and Tao [1] and uses color and texture histograms, which are widely used as features for human re-identification [1, 2, 12]. We first divide each image of a subject into six horizontal strips after rectifying the image as described in the previous section, so that the horizontal strips are parallel to the ground plane.

Since we want to re-identify human targets across different cameras, the color features used to represent the target should be invariant to lighting changes. Since RGB histograms are a poor choice [5], we use three histograms over the transformed RGB space defined as

$$(R', G', B') = \left(\frac{R - \mu_R}{\sigma_R}, \frac{G - \mu_G}{\sigma_G}, \frac{B - \mu_B}{\sigma_B}\right)$$

where $\mu_{\{R,G,B\}}$ and $\sigma_{\{R,G,B\}}$ are the mean and standard deviation of each color channel respectively. This transformation is only applied to the person rectangles.

HSV histograms are also known to be descriptive for re-id and stable to lighting changes; thus we also include one histogram of the hue multiplied by the saturation at each pixel (since hue becomes unstable near the gray axis and its certainty is inversely proportional to saturation).

To represent texture, we compute the histograms of responses at each pixel of a strip to 13 Schimid filters and eight Gabor filters [1]. Figure 2.4 shows an example of extracting texture features from an image. In total, 25 types of features (four color and 21 texture) are computed at each strip pixel. We then compute the histogram over each feature in the strip using 16 bins, resulting in a $25 \cdot 16 = 400$-dimensional descriptor for each strip.

However, a feature vector does not necessarily equal to the signature. As we all know that one's signature has to be discriminative and ideally unique, such as one's handwriting, fingerprints, and iris. Hence after extracting the feature vectors, the importance of each feature dimension has to be learned, i.e., metric learning. By analyzing the feature vectors in the training data set, higher weights will be assigned to features that are more discriminative while lower weight will be assigned to features that are less correlated to identities of different person.

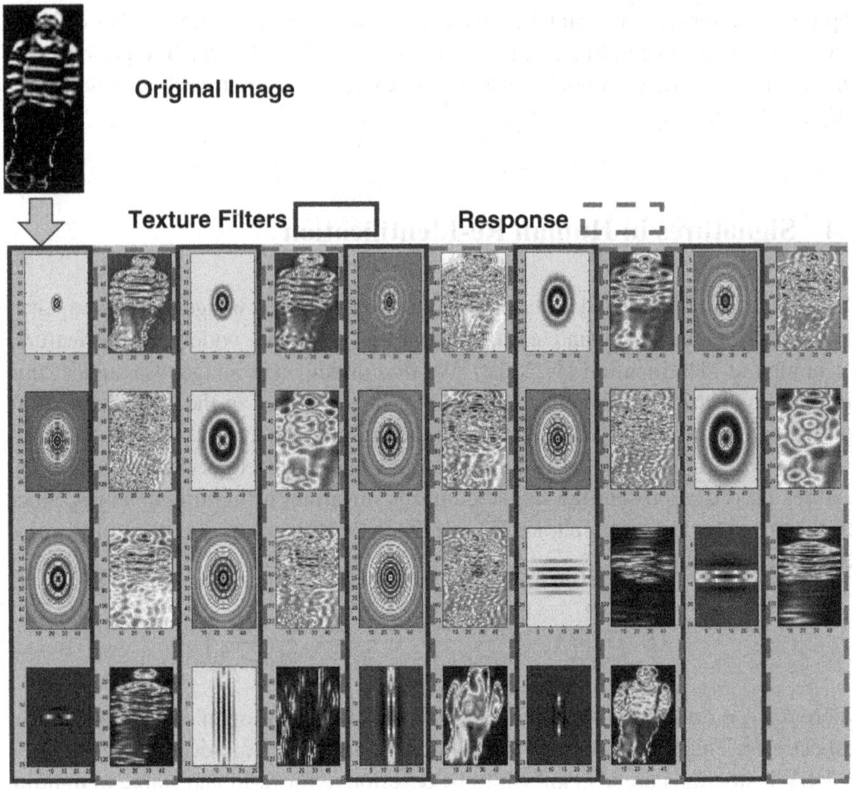

Fig. 2.4 An example of extracting texture features from an image

2.5 Discussion

In this chapter, we discuss about different types of visual features and the reasoning behind conventional features used in human re-identification problem. Finally, we briefly explained the difference between feature vectors and signatures.

References

1. C. Harris, M. Stephens, in *'A Combined Corner and Edge Detector*, 4th Alvey Vision Conference, (Manchester, UK, 1988)
2. J.A. Noble, Finding corners. Image Vis. Comput. **6**, 121–128 (1988)
3. J. Shi, C. Tomasi, Good features to track, in *IEEE Conference on Computer Vision and Pattern Recognition*, Seattle, WA, 1994
4. R.J. Radke, *Computer Vision for Visual Effects* (Cambridge University Press, Cambridge, UK, 2012)

5. E. Rosten, T. Drummond, *Fusing points and lines for high performance tracking*, in IEEE International Conference on Computer Vision, Beijing, China, 2005
6. E. Rosten, T. Drummond, *Machine learning for high-speed corner detection*, in European Conference on Computer Vision 2006, Graz, Austria, 2006
7. E. Rosten, R. Porter, T. Drummond, Faster and better: a machine learning approach to corner detection. IEEE Trans. Pattern Anal. Mach. Intell. **32**, 105–119 (2010)
8. D.G. Lowe, Distinctive image features from scale-invariant keypoints. Int. J. Comput. Vis. **60**, 91–110 (2004)
9. T. Lindeberg, Scale-space theory: a basic tool for analyzing structures at different scales. J. Appl. Stat. **21**(1), 225–270 (1994)
10. H. Bay, A. Ess, T. Tuytelaars, L. Van Gool, Speeded-up robust features (SURF). Comput. Vis. Imag. Underst. **110**(3), 346–359 (2008)
11. J. Luo, O. Gwun, A comparison of SIFT, PCA-SIFT and SURF. Int. J. Imag. Process. **3**, 143 (2009)
12. M. Calonder, V. Lepetit, C. Strecha, P. Fua, in *BRIEF: Binary Robust Independent Elementary Features*, European Conference on Computer Vision, (Heraklion, Crete, Greece, 2010)
13. E. Rublee, V. Rabaud, K. Konolige, G. Bradski, in *ORB: An efficient alternative to SIFT or SURF*, International Conference on Computer Vision (Barcelona, Spain, 2011)
14. S. Leutenegger, M. Chli, R.Y. Siegwart, in *BRISK: Binary Robust invariant scalable keypoints*, International Conference on Computer Vision (Barcelona, Spain, 2011)
15. A. Alahi, R. Ortiz, in *FREAK: Fast Retina Keypoint*, IEEE Conference on Computer Vision and Pattern Recognition, (Newport, RI, 2012)
16. B.K. Horn, B.G. Schunck, Determining optical flow. Artif. Intell. **17**, 185–203 (1981)

Chapter 3
Multi-object Tracking

We talked about how to obtain features of a sub-image in the previous chapter. In this chapter, we will discuss the approach to obtain the bounding box of each candidates from a raw video frame and maintain consistent identification for each person in a video sequence, that is, multi-object tracking.

3.1 Tracking

Tracking can be defined as finding the translation (u, v) of a patch of pixels at time t which corresponds to a patch of pixels p at time $t+1$. Horn and Schunk [1] proposed an optical flow method to generate dense flow fields by finding the flow vector at each pixel based on the brightness constancy constraint

$$I(x, y, t) = I(x + u, y + u, t + \Delta t). \tag{3.1}$$

Shi and Tomasi [2] proposed the Kanade–Lucas–Tomasi (KLT) tracker which computes an optical flow vector at pixel (x, y) by minimizing the cost function

$$c(u, v) = \sum_{(x,y)} w(x, y) \left(I(x + u, y + v, t + 1) - I(x, y, t)\right)^2 \tag{3.2}$$

in which $w(x, y)$ shares the same meaning as in Eq. (2.2). All the pixels in the patch are assumed to share the same motion vector. Using a Taylor series approximation, we have

Z. Wu, *Human Re-Identification*, Multimedia Systems and Applications,
DOI 10.1007/978-3-319-40991-7_3

$$\begin{bmatrix} \sum_{(x,y)} w(x,y) \left(\frac{\partial I(x,y)}{\partial x}\right)^2 & \sum_{(x,y)} w(x,y) \frac{\partial I(x,y)}{\partial x} \frac{\partial I(x,y)}{\partial y} \\ \sum_{(x,y)} w(x,y) \frac{\partial I(x,y)}{\partial x} \frac{\partial I(x,y)}{\partial y} & \sum_{(x,y)} w(x,y) \left(\frac{\partial I(x,y)}{\partial y}\right)^2 \end{bmatrix} \begin{bmatrix} u \\ v \end{bmatrix} \tag{3.3}$$

$$= - \begin{bmatrix} \sum_{(x,y)} w(x,y) \frac{\partial I(x,y)}{\partial x} \frac{\partial I(x,y)}{\partial t} \\ \sum_{(x,y)} w(x,y) \frac{\partial I(x,y)}{\partial y} \frac{\partial I(x,y)}{\partial t} \end{bmatrix}. \tag{3.4}$$

By solving this linear system, the minimum of Eq. (3.2) can be reached, and the quality of the tracked region can be obtained by finding the affine transformation between (x, y) and $(x + u, y + v)$ as

$$\begin{bmatrix} x + u \\ y + v \end{bmatrix} = \begin{bmatrix} a_1 & a_2 \\ a_3 & a_4 \end{bmatrix} \begin{bmatrix} x \\ y \end{bmatrix} + \begin{bmatrix} t_x \\ t_y \end{bmatrix}. \tag{3.5}$$

With the transformation, we can find the sum of squared differences between the patch in the current frame and the transformed patch in the previous frame. Then the tracker can decide to continue tracking this patch if the SSD is small or otherwise stop tracking the patch. The face region is defined, KLT corners are detected in the region, and they are then tracked through the other frames with the KLT tracker.

Another popular region tracking algorithm is Mean Shift Tracking proposed by Comaniciu et al. [3]. The object to be tracked is modeled and matched by color probability density functions estimated by Mean Shift. However, a fixed color distribution is used in Mean Shift tracking which is subject to change due to rotation in depth. The Continuous Adaptive Mean Shift (CAMSHIFT) algorithm proposed by Bradski [4] can handle changing color distributions by adaptively computing the size of the Mean Shift search window and estimating the color distribution in the search window.

3.2 Multiple-target Tracking

We usually want to track more than one object simultaneously in real-world scenarios of video surveillance. Although numerous object tracking methods have been proposed, when it comes to multiple object tracking, the problem is always much more complicated due to problems involving association such as occlusion. Most of the work of multiple object tracking is based on kernel tracking methods, more specifically appearance models. Some of these algorithms are based on current and past observations of the targets in order to estimate their current state, which are suitable for online applications. Breitenstein et al. [5] proposed a tracking-by-detection method to enable robust multiple-target human tracking based on a graded observation model trained online.

Other algorithms for multiple-target tracking take into account future information in estimating the current states of the objects [6–8]. While increasing latency in computation and association, ambiguities in association can be resolved more easily. Jiang et al. [9] proposed using linear programming to optimize the associations in multiple object tracking. The multiple object tracking problem is posed as a multiple-path searching problem which is especially designed to handle occlusion. A path is formed by a sequence of states including location and appearance information. Object layouts are constrained by penalty terms. For each object in each frame, there is an Occlusion Node accounting for the occluded object state when no other nonoverlapping location is available. This problem can be solved with a linear programming relaxation algorithm with acceptable computational load.

Recently, Benfold and Reid [10] introduced a robust real-time multi-target tracking system modeling the affinity between observations based on the Minimum Description Length Principle (MDL). An off-line trained Histogram of Oriented Gradients (HOG) [11] full-body human detector is used to detect objects. A pyramidal KLT tracker is used to track corner features and estimate motion of objects. Markov-Chain Monte-Carlo Data Association (MCMCDA) is used so that occlusion can be handled, and false alarms are allowed, which can be effectively identified and removed in the background. This system proved to be effective and computationally efficient.

3.3 Discussion

Object tracking is a crucial component in re-identification. Although it is not in the scope of most academic research papers on the topic of human re-identification, top priority should be given to this component when building a real-world re-identification system since only a good tracker can generate comprehensive and accurate candidates for the re-identification algorithms to process and match.

References

1. B.K. Horn, B.G. Schunck, Determining optical flow. Artif. Intell. **17**, 185–203 (1981). Aug
2. J. Shi, C. Tomasi, Good features to track, in *IEEE Conference on Computer Vision and Pattern Recognition*, Seattle, WA, 1994
3. D. Comaniciu, V. Ramesh, P. Meer, Real-time tracking of non-rigid objects using mean shift, in *IEEE Conference on Computer Vision and Pattern Recognition 2000*, vol. 2, Atlantic City, NJ, 2000
4. G.R. Bradski, Computer Vision Face Tracking For Use in a Perceptual User Interface. in *IEEE Workshop on Applications of Computer Vision*, Princeton, NJ, 1998
5. M.D. Breitenstein, F. Reichlin, B. Leibe, E. Koller-Meier, L. Van Gool, Robust tracking-by-detection using a detector confidence particle filter. in *IEEE International Conference on Computer Vision*, Kyoto, Japan, 2009
6. C. Huang, B. Wu, R. Nevatia, Robust object tracking by hierarchical association of detection responses, in *European Conference on Computer Vision*, Marseille, France, 2008
7. B. Leibe, K. Schindler, L. Van Gool, Coupled detection and trajectory estimation for multi-object tracking, in *Internatiobal Conference on Computer Vision*, Rio de Janeiro, Brazil, 2007

8. Y. Li, C. Huang, R. Nevatia, Learning to associate: HybridBoosted multi-target tracker for crowded scene, in *IEEE Conference on Computer Vision and Pattern Recognition*, Miami, FL, June 2009
9. H. Jiang, S. Fels, J. Little, A linear programming approach for multiple object tracking, in *IEEE Conference on Computer Vision and Pattern Recognition*, Minneapolis, MN, 2007
10. B. Benfold, I. Reid, Stable multi-target tracking in real-time surveillance video, in *IEEE Conference on Computer Vision and Pattern Recognition 2011*, Colorado Springs, CO, 2011
11. N. Dalal, B. Triggs, C. Schmid, Human detection using oriented histograms of flow and appearance, in *European Conference on Computer Vision*, Graz, Austria, 2006

Part II
Camera Network and Infrastructures Planning

In the second part of this book, we are going to talk about the infrastructures planning and design for real-world human re-identification applications. The planning of infrastructures includes the choice of cameras, the network communication mechanism, and the accurate spatial calibration of the camera network. The prior information of the camera network, which is usually ignored by lab researches, is in fact very valuable and useful in practice.

Chapter 4
Surveillance Camera and Its Calibration

4.1 Camera Calibration

Camera calibration is an essential prerequisite for many computer vision applications, and it is also the first step in order to obtain metric information from images. For more than a century, camera calibration has been a key process and research hotspot for photogrammetry. Roelofs [1] summarizes popular camera calibration techniques during the period of 1880–1950s. Since the burgeoning of computer vision in 1960s, many modern camera calibration methods based on pinhole camera model have been proposed, which can be classified into two main categories: classic calibration and self-calibration.

For classic calibration, objects with accurately measured or manufactured features need to be used to provide points reference, which we call calibration targets. Sometimes, a controlled scene is used instead of a calibration target or fiducial markers. By taking pictures of the target with the camera and extracting the features from the images, the parameters of the camera model can be recovered. Self-calibration methods, also referred as auto-calibration, determine intrinsic camera parameters without using any calibration target.

Camera calibration may not sound relevant to human re-identification. However if one wants to build a real-world solution for human re-identification, he/she has to understand the cameras.

4.2 Camera Model

Usually, a pinhole model is used to model a camera. A 3D point $\mathbf{X}$ and its image projection $\mathbf{x}$ are related by

$$s\widetilde{\mathbf{x}} = \mathbf{K}\,[\mathbf{R} \mid \mathbf{t}]\,\widetilde{\mathbf{X}} \tag{4.1}$$

Z. Wu, *Human Re-Identification*, Multimedia Systems and Applications,
DOI 10.1007/978-3-319-40991-7_4

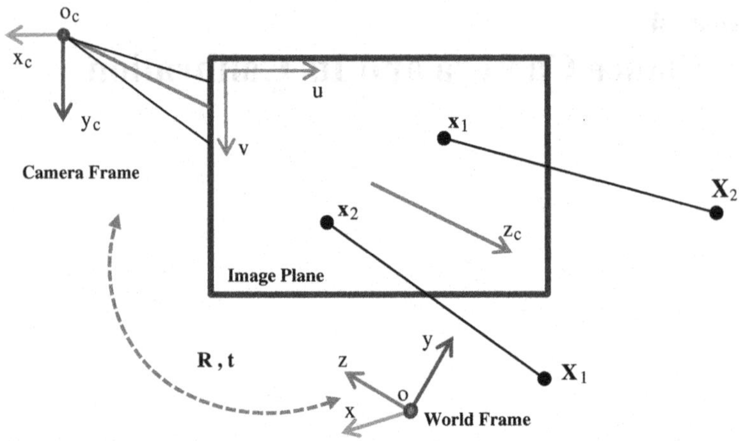

Fig. 4.1 Pinhole model of a camera

in which **K** is a 3 × 3 calibration matrix given by

$$\mathbf{K} = \begin{bmatrix} f_x & \gamma & c_x \\ 0 & f_y & c_y \\ 0 & 0 & 1 \end{bmatrix} \tag{4.2}$$

where f_x and f_y are the focal length in units of x and y pixel dimension and $\mathbf{c} = (c_x, c_y)$ is the principal point on image frame. s is an arbitrary scale factor, and γ is the skewness of the two image axes. **R** and **t** are the 3 × 3 rotation matrix and 3 × 1 translation vector that specify the external parameters of the camera, and $\widetilde{x}$ and $\widetilde{X}$ are the homogeneous coordinates of the image projection and 3D point, respectively. The camera model is illustrated in Fig. 4.1.

4.3 Distortion Model

Real-world camera-lens systems do not satisfy the ideal pinhole model. One of the most important factors is that lenses bring distortions, among which radial and tangential distortion have been discussed most. Brown [2] introduced a model to represent both radial and tangential (decentering) distortion given by

$$\begin{aligned} x_u &= c_x + (x_d - c_x)(1 + \kappa_1 r^2 + \kappa_2 r^4 + \cdots) \\ y_u &= c_y + (y_d - c_y)(1 + \kappa_1 r^2 + \kappa_2 r^4 + \cdots) \end{aligned} \tag{4.3}$$

in which

$$r = \sqrt{(x_d - c_x)^2 + (x_d - c_y)^2}. \tag{4.4}$$

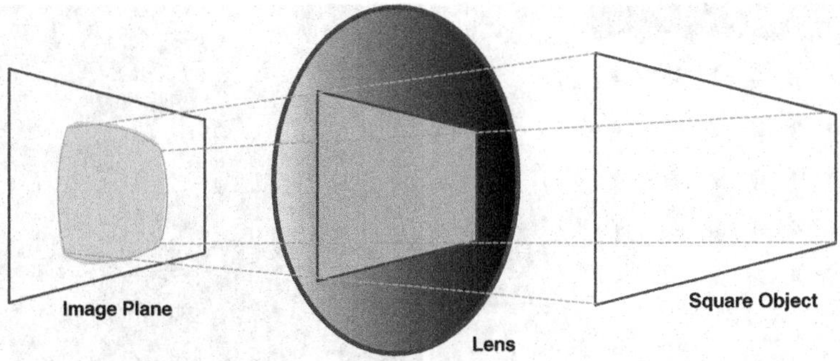

Fig. 4.2 Illustration of radial distortion

(x_u, y_u) are the undistorted image coordinates and (x_d, y_d) are the distorted image coordinates. $(\kappa_1, \kappa_2, \dots, \kappa_n)$ are the distortion coefficients. Due to the improvement of the manufacturing quality of optical lenses, tangential distortion in lenses is becoming smaller and smaller, so that we usually completely ignore tangential distortion in practice. Figure 4.2 illustrates how the radial distortion affects the projection of a square object on the image plane.

Usually, distortion coefficients are estimated during camera calibration through nonlinear optimization together with other camera parameters, though various methods have been proposed to estimate them independently [3–6]. Once $\kappa_1, \kappa_2, \dots, \kappa_n$ are obtained, distortion can be corrected from distorted images with Eq. (4.3).

4.4 Calibrating Cameras with 3D Targets

Camera calibration with known 3D targets is one of the earliest proposed calibration approaches. Some of the 3D targets used in machine vision applications (e.g., vision inspection) are usually very expensive, since they are either precisely manufactured or precisely measured [7]. Figure 4.3 shows an example of a 3D target.

The world frame is defined with respect to the target; that is, the correspondences between $\mathbf{x}$ and $\mathbf{X}$ are known. The camera matrix

$$\mathbf{P} = \mathbf{K}\,[\mathbf{R} \mid \mathbf{t}] \tag{4.5}$$

can be determined by the Direct Linear Transform (DLT) [8] as follows. With 3D points to 2D projection correspondences $(\mathbf{X}_i, \mathbf{x}_i)$, we have

$$\mathbf{x}_i = \mathbf{P}\mathbf{X}_i. \tag{4.6}$$

Note that $(\mathbf{X}_i, \mathbf{x}_i)$ are homogeneous coordinates, hence it can be rewritten as the vector cross product

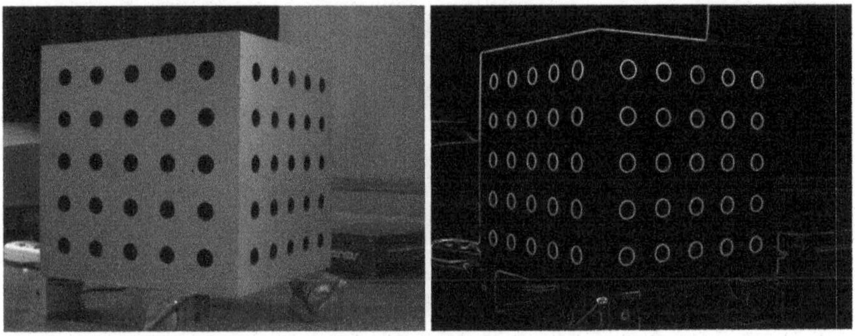

Fig. 4.3 A 3D target for camera calibration with circular feature points

$$\mathbf{x}_i \times \mathbf{P}\mathbf{X}_i = 0 \tag{4.7}$$

in which $\mathbf{X}_i$ and $\mathbf{x}_i$ are 3×1 vectors and $\mathbf{P}$ is a 3×3 matrix. Let $\mathbf{x}_i = [\, u_i \ v_i \ w_i \,]^\top$, we have

$$\mathbf{x}_i \times \mathbf{P}\mathbf{X}_i \tag{4.8}$$

$$= \begin{bmatrix} u_i \\ v_i \\ w_i \end{bmatrix} \times \begin{bmatrix} \mathbf{p}_1\mathbf{X}_i \\ \mathbf{p}_2\mathbf{X}_i \\ \mathbf{p}_3\mathbf{X}_i \end{bmatrix} \tag{4.9}$$

$$= \begin{bmatrix} v_i\mathbf{p}_3\mathbf{X}_i - w_i\mathbf{p}_2\mathbf{X}_i \\ w_i\mathbf{p}_1\mathbf{X}_i - u_i\mathbf{p}_3\mathbf{X}_i \\ u_i\mathbf{p}_2\mathbf{X}_i - v_i\mathbf{p}_1\mathbf{X}_i \end{bmatrix} \tag{4.10}$$

$$= \begin{bmatrix} \mathbf{0} & -w_i\mathbf{X}_i^\top & v_i\mathbf{X}_i^\top \\ w_i\mathbf{X}_i^\top & \mathbf{0} & -u_i\mathbf{X}_i^\top \\ -v_i\mathbf{X}_i^\top & u_i\mathbf{X}_i^\top & \mathbf{0} \end{bmatrix} \begin{bmatrix} \mathbf{p}_1 \\ \mathbf{p}_2 \\ \mathbf{p}_3 \end{bmatrix} \tag{4.11}$$

$$=0 \tag{4.12}$$

in which $\mathbf{p}_i$ is the ith row of $\mathbf{P}$. Equation (4.12) can be seen as an

$$\mathbf{A}\mathbf{b} = 0 \tag{4.13}$$

problem, in which we have two independent equations in 11 unknowns. The vector

$$\mathbf{b} = \left[\mathbf{p}_1 \ \mathbf{p}_2 \ \mathbf{p}_3\right]^\top \tag{4.14}$$

can be determined using more than six correspondences by minimizing $\|\mathbf{A}\mathbf{b}\|$ subject to

$$\|\mathbf{b}\| = 1. \tag{4.15}$$

The intrinsic parameters can be recovered by

$$c_x = \frac{b_1 b_9 + b_2 b_{10} + b_3 b_{11}}{b_9^2 + b_{10}^2 + b_{11}^2} \tag{4.16}$$

$$c_y = \frac{b_5 b_9 + b_6 b_{10} + b_7 b_{11}}{b_9^2 + b_{10}^2 + b_{11}^2} \tag{4.17}$$

$$f_x = \sqrt{-c_x^2 + \frac{b_1^2 + b_2^2 + b_3^2}{(b_9^2 + b_{10}^2 + b_{11}^2)^2}} \tag{4.18}$$

$$f_x = \sqrt{-c_y^2 + \frac{b_5^2 + b_6^2 + b_7^2}{(b_9^2 + b_{10}^2 + b_{11}^2)^2}}. \tag{4.19}$$

However, the DLT only solves for a set of parameters of a linear system without considering the dependency among parameters, and distortion from lenses will induce serious error to the calibration results.

Tsai [9] proposed the Radial Alignment Constraint (RAC), which is a function of the relative rotation and translation between the camera and the feature points on the target when solving for camera intrinsic and extrinsic parameters, followed by nonlinear optimization to find the distortion parameters. With the RAC, camera calibration can reach a higher accuracy since the error from lens distortion in the scale factors and the distance from the camera to the origin of the world frame are eliminated, resulting a better initial guess for both external and internal parameters.

Camera calibration can usually achieve high accuracy with algorithms in this category. However, these methods usually require expensive calibration targets, which makes them hard to apply in practical applications.

4.5 Calibrating Cameras with Planar Targets

Tsai [9] also introduced a method to calibrate a camera with a planar target. However, this method requires that the planar target precisely undergoes known pure translational movement, which can be considered in a way as a known 3D target as well. Zhang [10] proposed an algorithm to calibrate a camera with an unconstrained planar target. An example of such a planar target is shown in Figs. 4.4 and 4.5.

The target plane is set to $Z = 0$ in the world frame. Equation (4.1) becomes

$$s\widetilde{\mathbf{x}} = \mathbf{K} \begin{bmatrix} \mathbf{r}_1 & \mathbf{r}_2 & \mathbf{t} \end{bmatrix} \widetilde{\mathbf{X}} = \mathbf{H}\widetilde{\mathbf{X}} \tag{4.20}$$

in which $\mathbf{r}_1$ and $\mathbf{r}_2$ are the first and second columns of $\mathbf{R}$, and $\mathbf{H} = \begin{bmatrix} \mathbf{h}_1 & \mathbf{h}_2 & \mathbf{h}_3 \end{bmatrix}$ is the homography matrix between the target plane and the camera image plane. From Eq. 4.20, we have,

$$\mathbf{H} = \mathbf{K} \begin{bmatrix} \mathbf{r}_1 & \mathbf{r}_2 & \mathbf{t} \end{bmatrix}. \tag{4.21}$$

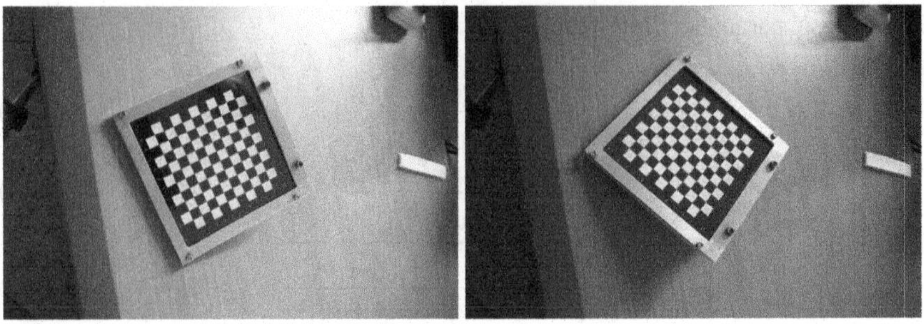

Fig. 4.4 Images used in camera calibration with a planar target

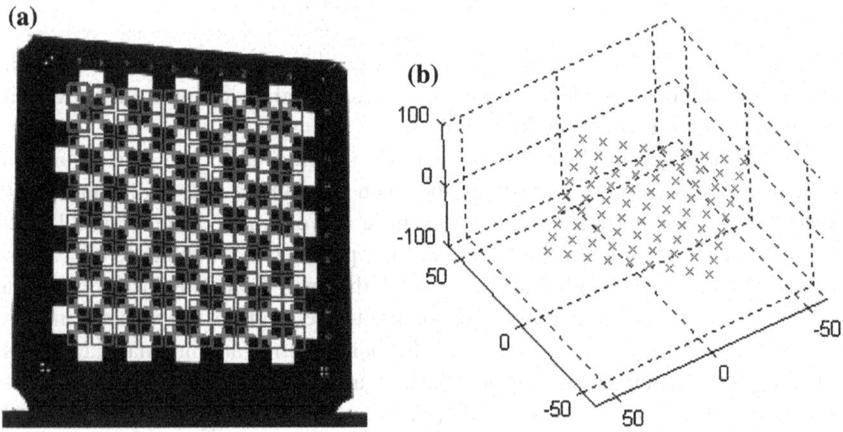

Fig. 4.5 Calibration with planar targets. **a** Feature points extracted on the checkerboard target. **b** Illustration of reconstructed feature points of the checkerboard target

Since $\mathbf{r}_1$ and $\mathbf{r}_2$ are orthonormal, two constraints can be obtained:

$$\mathbf{h}_1^\top \mathbf{K}^{-\top}\mathbf{K}^{-1}\mathbf{h}_2 = 0 \tag{4.22}$$

$$\mathbf{h}_1^\top \mathbf{K}^{-\top}\mathbf{K}^{-1}\mathbf{h}_1 = \mathbf{h}_2^\top \mathbf{K}^{-\top}\mathbf{K}^{-1}\mathbf{h}_2. \tag{4.23}$$

Let $\mathbf{B} = \mathbf{K}^{-\top}\mathbf{K}^{-1}$; this is a 3×3 matrix called the image of the absolute conic. We have

$$\mathbf{h}_i^\top \mathbf{B}\mathbf{h}_j = \begin{bmatrix} h_{i1}h_{j1} \\ h_{i1}h_{j2} + h_{i2}h_{j1} \\ h_{i2}h_{j2} \\ h_{i3}h_{j1} + h_{i1}h_{j3} \\ h_{i3}h_{j2} + h_{i2}h_{j3} \\ h_{i3}h_{j3} \end{bmatrix}^\top \begin{bmatrix} B_{11} \\ B_{12} \\ B_{22} \\ B_{13} \\ B_{23} \\ B_{33} \end{bmatrix} = \mathbf{v}_{ij}^\top \mathbf{b} = 0 \tag{4.24}$$

in which $\mathbf{v}_{ij}$ is a 6×1 vector constructed from elements of $\mathbf{h}_i$ and $\mathbf{h}_j$, and $\mathbf{b}$ is a 6×1 vector constructed from elements of $\mathbf{B}$. Similarly, with Eq. (4.23), we get

$$\begin{bmatrix} \mathbf{v}_{12}^\top \\ \mathbf{v}_{11}^\top - \mathbf{v}_{22}^\top \end{bmatrix} \mathbf{b} = 0. \tag{4.25}$$

Thus with more than three views of the target, we can solve for $\mathbf{b}$, and all the intrinsic and extrinsic parameters of the camera can be recovered as

$$c_y = \frac{b_2 b_4 - b_1 b_5}{b_1 b_3 - b_2^2} \tag{4.26}$$

$$\lambda = b_6 - \frac{b_4^2 + c_y(b_2 b_4 - b_1 b_5)}{b_1} \tag{4.27}$$

$$f_x = \sqrt{\frac{\lambda}{b_1}} \tag{4.28}$$

$$f_y = \sqrt{\lambda \frac{b_1}{b_1 b_3 - b_2^2}} \tag{4.29}$$

$$\gamma = -b_2 f_x^2 \frac{f_y}{\lambda} \tag{4.30}$$

$$c_x = \gamma \frac{c_y}{f_x} - b_4 \frac{f_x^2}{\lambda} \tag{4.31}$$

in which λ is an intermediate variable. Note that the extrinsic parameters are different for each view, which are used to generate 3D–2D projection constraints in the nonlinear optimization. When the skewless constraint is assumed ($\gamma = 0$), only two views are required to reach a unique solution. Distortion coefficients can also be retrieved by including the distortion model in the 3D–2D projection constraints in the nonlinear optimization.

Sturm and Maybank [11] proposed a similar algorithm with a simplified camera model and exhaustively studied degenerate cases of the algorithm. Similar algorithms based on a planar scene have been proposed by Liebowitz and Zisserman [12].

Plane-based camera calibration has become popular since this research, due to its high accuracy and good flexibility. Bouguet [13] released a popular camera calibration toolbox for MATLAB. With a printed checkerboard target, a camera can be calibrated in minutes.

4.6 Calibrating Cameras with 1D Targets

Plane-based camera calibration is effective. However, in some specific scenarios, a planar target may not be a good choice. For example, in applications involving large fields of view (FOVs), in order to reach reasonable calibration accuracy, the planar target should be manufactured at a large size (approximately 20 % of the area of the FOV), which may be very difficult. Also, when calibrating multiple cameras simultaneously, planar targets or 3D targets will impose serious occlusion/visibility problems.

Zhang [14] proposed a camera calibration method based on 1D targets. These 1D targets containing more than three colinear points move arbitrarily with one end fixed. The world frame is set to coincide with the camera frame. The known length of the target and the ratio between each pair of feature points form constraints on the intrinsic parameters. With more than six observations of the target, the internal parameters of the camera can be solved in closed form. The fixed point of the target need not be visible in the images, but each observation of the target needs to be independent to avoid singularities.

Similar work has been proposed to extend and improve calibration with 1D targets [15–20]. However, generally speaking, the calibration accuracy of 1D target-based algorithms is lower than plane-based and 3D targets. Plane-based calibration algorithms still dominate applications requiring classical calibration.

4.7 Self-calibration

Self-calibration does not require any calibration apparatus. Some self-calibration algorithms recover the multi-view poses of the camera by epipolar constraints or estimating fundamental matrices using correspondences from the scene [21, 22]. Others are based on cameras undergoing pure rotation [23–29], pure translation [30], or general motion under certain conditions [31]. Many of these algorithms involve solving Kruppa's Equation with the constraints from the absolute conic [8]. Also, some algorithms detect parallel lines in the scene and estimate the camera matrix from vanishing points [32–36].

Here, we review one self-calibration matrix based on camera rotation. Let $\mathbf{x}$ and $\mathbf{x}'$ be a pair of correspondences induced by the images of a 3D point $\mathbf{X}$ taken at two different instants by a camera undergoing unknown pure rotation. We have

$$\begin{aligned} \mathbf{x} &\sim \mathbf{KRX} \\ \mathbf{x}' &\sim \mathbf{K}'\mathbf{R}'\mathbf{X} \end{aligned} \tag{4.32}$$

in which $\mathbf{R}$ and $\mathbf{R}'$ are the rotation matrices corresponding to the two poses respectively. We can rewrite Eq. (4.32) as

$$\mathbf{x}' = \mathbf{K}'\mathbf{R}'\mathbf{R}^{-1}\mathbf{K}^{-1}\mathbf{x}. \tag{4.33}$$

In the case of constant focal length, the intrinsic matrix **K** remains the same, so we have

$$\mathbf{x}' = \mathbf{K}\mathbf{R}'\mathbf{R}^{-1}\mathbf{K}^{-1}\mathbf{x} = \mathbf{K}\mathbf{R}_\mathbf{r}\mathbf{K}^{-1}\mathbf{x}. \tag{4.34}$$

Let $\mathbf{B} = \mathbf{K}\mathbf{R}_\mathbf{r}\mathbf{K}^{-1}$, we have $\mathbf{x}' = \mathbf{B}\mathbf{x}$ and

$$\mathbf{K}\mathbf{K}^\mathbf{T} = \mathbf{B}\mathbf{K}\mathbf{K}^\mathbf{T}\mathbf{B}^\mathbf{T}. \tag{4.35}$$

Thus we can express the Image of the Absolute Conic (IAC) [8], given by $\Omega = (\mathbf{K}\mathbf{K}^\mathbf{T})^{-1}$, as:

$$\Omega = \left(\mathbf{K}\mathbf{K}^\mathbf{T}\right)^{-1} = \mathbf{B}_\mathbf{ji}^{-\mathbf{T}}\Omega\mathbf{B}_\mathbf{ji}^{-1} = \mathbf{B}_\mathbf{j0}^{-\mathbf{T}}\Omega\mathbf{B}_\mathbf{j0}^{-1}. \tag{4.36}$$

Here, Ω is a 3×3 matrix, $i, j = 0, 1, \ldots, N$ are the indexes of images used in the calibration, and we can explicitly write

$$\Omega = f_x^{-2}\begin{bmatrix} 1 & 0 & -c_x \\ 0 & \frac{1}{\alpha^2} & \frac{-c_y}{\alpha^2} \\ -c_x & \frac{-c_y}{\alpha^2} & f_x^2 + c_x^2 + \frac{c_y^2}{\alpha^2} \end{bmatrix} \tag{4.37}$$

in which $\alpha = \frac{f_y}{f_x}$. We write (4.36) in the form $\mathbf{Ab} = \mathbf{0}$ where **A** is a $6m \times 6$ matrix and **b** contains the elements of ω rearranged as a 6×1 vector. We solve for ω and obtain K using the Cholesky decomposition of ω using (4.36). Then we can obtain

$$\mathbf{R}^\mathbf{i} = \mathbf{K}^{-1}\mathbf{H}^\mathbf{i}\mathbf{K}. \tag{4.38}$$

The intrinsic matrix **K** can be refined by minimizing

$$\sum_{i=2}^{m}\sum_{j=1}^{n} d(\mathbf{x}_\mathbf{j}^\mathbf{i}, \mathbf{K}\mathbf{R}^\mathbf{i}\mathbf{x}_\mathbf{j}^\mathbf{1})^2 \tag{4.39}$$

over **K** and $\mathbf{R}^\mathbf{i}$. x_j^1, x_j^i are the image positions of the jth matched feature measured in the first and the ith images, respectively. Self-calibration approaches usually can only obtain intrinsic camera parameters and limited/relative extrinsic parameters such as rotation angles.

Self-calibration methods are very flexible, but suffer in calibration accuracy due to the assumptions or constraints for the algorithm not being perfectly satisfied (e.g., the pure rotation assumption is usually violated due to translational offsets [37]). According to error analysis [37, 38], the accuracy of self-calibration algorithms is usually much lower than that of classic calibration. Some algorithms cannot recover all parameters or need to adapt simplified camera models. Nevertheless, self-calibration algorithms are widely used in wide-area surveillance and robot vision applications due to their high flexibility and apparatus-independent nature.

4.8 Discussion

In this chapter, we introduce the basic concepts of camera calibration. Camera calibration may not seem relevant to conventional human re-identification research, but it is playing a very important role in making the real-world re-identification to work. In later chapter, we will discuss in detail how to make use of calibration information in boosting the performance of metric learning.

References

1. R. Roelofs, Distortion, principal point, point of symmetry and calibrated principal point. Photogrammetria **7**, 49–66 (1951)
2. D.C. Brown, Decentering distortion of lenses. Photom. Eng. **32**(3), 444–462 (1966)
3. G. Stein, Lens distortion calibration using point correspondences, in *IEEE Conference on Computer Vision and Pattern Recognition*, San Juan, PR, 1997
4. F. Devernay, O.D. Faugeras, Automatic calibration and removal of distortion from scenes of structured environments. Proc. SPIE **2567**, 62–72 (1995)
5. R. Swaminathan, S. Nayar, Nonmetric calibration of wide-angle lenses and polycameras. IEEE Trans. Pattern Anal. Mach. Intell. **22**, 1172–1178 (2000)
6. J.P. Tardif, P. Sturm, M. Trudeau, S. Roy, Calibration of cameras with radially symmetric distortion. IEEE Trans. Pattern Anal. Mach. Intell. **31**, 1552–1566 (2009)
7. Z. Wu, Research on Calibration of Stereo Vision Sensor in Large FOV, M.S. thesis, Department of Measurement, Control and Information Technology, Beihang Univ., Beijing, China, 2009
8. R. Hartley, A. Zisserman, *Multiple View Geometry in Computer Vision*, 2nd edn. (Cambridge University Press, Cambridge, 2004)
9. R.Y. Tsai, A versatile camera calibration technique for high-accuracy 3D machine vision metrology using off-the-shelf TV cameras and lenses. IEEE J. Robot. Autom. **3**, 323–344 (1987)
10. Z. Zhang, A flexible new technique for camera calibration. IEEE Trans. Pattern Anal. Mach. Intell. **22**, 1330–1334 (2000)
11. P. Sturm, S. Maybank, On plane-based camera calibration: a general algorithm, singularities, applications, in *IEEE Conference on Computer Vision and Pattern Recognition*, Fort Collins, CO, 1999
12. D. Liebowitz, A. Zisserman, Metric rectification for perspective images of planes, in *IEEE Conference on Computer Vision and Pattern Recognition*, Santa Barbara, CA, 1998
13. J.Y. Bouguet, Camera Calibration Toolbox (online) (2 December 2013), http://www.vision.caltech.edu/bouguetj/calib_doc/. Accessed 15 Jan 2014
14. Z. Zhang, Camera calibration with one-dimensional objects. IEEE Trans. Pattern Anal. Mach. Intell. **26**, 892–899 (2004)
15. P. Hammarstedt, P. Sturm, A. Heyden, Degenerate cases and closed-form solutions for camera calibration with one-dimensional objects, in *IEEE International Conference on Computer Vision*, Beijing, China, 2005

16. I. Miyagawa, H. Arai, H. Koike, Simple camera calibration from a single image using five points on two orthogonal 1-D objects. IEEE Trans. Image Process. **19**, 1528–1538 (2010)
17. E. Peng, L. Li, Camera calibration using one-dimensional information and its applications in both controlled and uncontrolled environments. Pattern Recognit. **43**, 1188–1198 (2010)
18. F. Qi, Q. Li, Y. Luo, D. Hu, Constraints on general motions for camera calibration with one-dimensional objects. Pattern Recognit. **40**, 1785–1792 (2007)
19. F. Qi, Q. Li, Y. Luo, D. Hu, Camera calibration with one-dimensional objects moving under gravity. Pattern Recognit. **40**, 343–345 (2007)
20. L. Wang, F.C. Wu, Z.Y. Hu, Multi-camera calibration with one-dimensional object under general motions, in IEEE *International Conference on Computer Vision*, Rio de Janeiro, Brazil, 2007
21. S.J. Maybank, O.D. Faugeras, A theory of self-calibration of a moving camera. Int. J. Comput. Vis. **8**, 123–151 (1992)
22. Q. Luong, O. Faugeras, Self-calibration of a moving camera from point correspondences and fundamental matrices. Intl. J. Comput. Vis. **22**(3), 261–289 (1997)
23. L. Agapito, E. Hayman, I. Reid, Self-calibration of rotating and zooming cameras. Intl. J. Comput. Vis. **45**, 107–127 (2001)
24. G. Stein, Accurate internal camera calibration using rotation, with analysis of sources of error, in *IEEE International Conference on Computer Vision*, Boston, US, 1995
25. J. Oh, K. Sohn, Semiautomatic zoom lens calibration based on the camera's rotation. J. Electron. Imaging **20**, 023006 (2011)
26. J.M. Frahm, R. Koch, Camera calibration with known rotation, in *IEEE International Conference on Computer Vision*, Madison, WI, 2003
27. C. Li, J. Lu, L. Ma, Improved rotation-based self-calibration with a strategy of rotational angles. Opt. Eng. **48**, 097202 (2009)
28. R.I. Hartley, Self-calibration of stationary cameras. Intl. J. Comput. Vis. **22**, 5–23 (1997)
29. Q. Ji, S. Dai, Self-calibration of a rotating camera with a translational offset. IEEE Trans. Robot. Autom. **20**, 1–14 (2004)
30. S. Ma, A self-calibration technique for active vision systems. IEEE Trans. Robot. Autom. **12**, 114–120 (1996)
31. M. Pollefeys, R. Koch, L. Gool, Self-calibration and metric reconstruction inspite of varying and unknown intrinsic camera parameters. Int. J. Comput. Vis. **32**(1), 7–25 (1999)
32. B. Caprile, V. Torre, Using vanishing points for camera calibration. Int. J. Comput. Vis. **4**, 127–139 (1990)
33. B. He, Y. Li, Camera calibration with lens distortion and from vanishing points. Opt. Eng. **48**, 013603 (2009)
34. L. Grammatikopoulos, G. Karras, E. Petsa, An automatic approach for camera calibration from vanishing points. ISPRS J. Photogramm. Remote Sens. **62**, 64–76 (2007)
35. B. He, Y. Li, Camera calibration from vanishing points in a vision system. Opt. Laser Technol. **40**, 555–561 (2008)
36. Z. Zhao, Y. Liu, Z. Zhang, Camera calibration with three noncollinear points under special motions. IEEE Trans. Image Process. **17**, 2393–2402 (2008)
37. L. Wang, S.B. Kang, H.-Y. Shum, G. Xu, Error analysis of pure rotation-based self-calibration. IEEE Trans. Pattern Anal. Mach. Intell. **26**, 275–280 (2004)
38. B. Tordoff, D. Murray, The impact of radial distortion on the self-calibration of rotating cameras. Comput. Vis. Image Underst. **96**, 17–34 (2004)

Chapter 5
Calibrating a Surveillance Camera Network

In principal, human re-identification is essentially a cross-camera tracking problem. In other words, human re-identification systems are deployed in the environment that has a camera network, such as airports, public transportation stations, and office buildings. In this chapter, we are going to talk about the setup and calibration of a surveillance camera network.

5.1 Related Work

The calibration of camera network is similar to calibrating a stereo rig, which can be defined as estimating the external parameter (i.e., relative position), or so-called structure parameters between cameras. Assuming the relative position between two cameras are fixed, the internal parameter and external parameters of the stereo rig can be obtained with one shot. With a planar target, after calculating the internal parameters of each camera, the structure parameters can be found with one shot of the target with Zhang's method [1]. Zhang et al. [2] proposed a self-calibration method for camera network based on point correspondences. Hartley [3] proposed eight-point algorithm in estimating fundamental matrix, from which structure parameters can be extracted. Devarajan et al. [4] proposed several practical algorithms in calibrating distributed camera network based on vision graph and belief propagation. Sinha and Pollefeys [5] proposed synchronizing and calibrating camera network from tracking silhouettes. Rahimi et al. [6] introduced a method that simultaneously calibrate and track objects with a camera with nonoverlapping FOV based on the prior knowledge about target's dynamics.

Z. Wu, *Human Re-Identification*, Multimedia Systems and Applications,
DOI 10.1007/978-3-319-40991-7_5

5.2 Camera Network

In order to relate the cameras' images to each other, all cameras in the network must be jointly calibrated.

Let **K** be the intrinsic parameter matrix of a camera, given by

$$\mathbf{K} = \begin{bmatrix} f_x & 0 & c_x \\ 0 & f_y & c_y \\ 0 & 0 & 1 \end{bmatrix} \tag{5.1}$$

in which c_x, c_y is the principal point, f_x and f_y are the focal length in the units of x and y pixel dimension. We have

$$\lambda \mathbf{p} = \lambda \begin{bmatrix} u \\ v \\ 1 \end{bmatrix} = \mathbf{M} \begin{bmatrix} x \\ y \\ z \\ 1 \end{bmatrix} = \mathbf{K}(\mathbf{RP} + \mathbf{t}) \tag{5.2}$$

in which $\mathbf{p}$ is the homogeneous coordinate of a point (u, v) on the image plane, $\mathbf{P} = (x, y, z)$ is the 3D coordinate of the corresponding point in the environment, λ is a scalar, and $\mathbf{M}$ is the camera calibration matrix, comprised of the internal parameter matrix $\mathbf{K}$, the rotation matrix $\mathbf{R}$, and the translation vector $\mathbf{t}$.

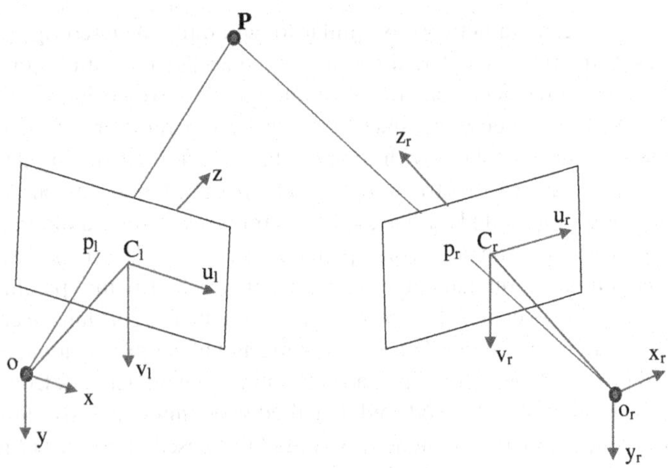

Fig. 5.1 Model of a stereo rig

When we have a stereo camera pair, shown in Fig. 5.1 let $\mathbf{K_l}$ and $\mathbf{K_r}$ be the intrinsic matrix for left and right cameras respectively. The extrinsic parameters between the two cameras are

$$\lambda_l \mathbf{p}_l = \mathbf{K}_l \left[\mathbf{I} \; \mathbf{0} \right] \mathbf{P} = \mathbf{M}_l \mathbf{P} \tag{5.3}$$

$$\lambda_r \mathbf{p}_r = \mathbf{K}_r \left[\mathbf{R} \; \mathbf{t} \right] \mathbf{P} = \mathbf{M}_r \mathbf{P} \tag{5.4}$$

in which $\mathbf{M}_l$ and $\mathbf{M}_r$ are the projection matrices for left and right cameras respectively. Then we have

$$\begin{bmatrix} u_l m^l_{31} - m^l_{11} & u_l m^l_{32} - m^l_{11} & u_l m^l_{33} - m^l_{13} \\ v_l m^l_{31} - m^l_{21} & v_l m^l_{32} - m^l_{22} & v_l m^l_{33} - m^l_{23} \\ u_r m^r_{31} - m^r_{11} & u_r m^r_{31} - m^r_{12} & u_r m^r_{33} - m^r_{13} \\ v_r m^r_{31} - m^r_{21} & v_r m^r_{31} - m^r_{22} & v_r m^r_{33} - m^r_{23} \end{bmatrix} \begin{bmatrix} x \\ y \\ z \end{bmatrix} = \begin{bmatrix} m^l_{14} - u_l m^l_{34} \\ m^l_{24} - v_l m^l_{34} \\ m^r_{14} - u_r m^r_{34} \\ m^r_{24} - v_r m^r_{34} \end{bmatrix} \tag{5.5}$$

in which m_{ij} is the element in the ith row and jth column of $\mathbf{M}_{\{l,r\}}$. $\mathbf{p}_l(u_l, v_l)$ and $\mathbf{p}_r(u_r, v_r)$ are the projection of $\mathbf{P}$ on image planes of left and right camera respectively. Also, radial distortion from the lens is considered in the calibration

$$u_u = (u_d - c_x)(1 + \kappa_1 r^2 + \kappa_2 r^4) \tag{5.6}$$

$$v_u = (v_d - c_y)(1 + \kappa_1 r^2 + \kappa_2 r^4) \tag{5.7}$$

in which

$$r = \sqrt{(u_d - c_x)^2 + (v_d - c_y)^2} \tag{5.8}$$

where (u_u, v_u) is the undistorted image coordinates and (u_d, v_d) is the distorted image coordinates. κ_1 and κ_2 are the distortion coefficients.

5.3 Calibrating Intrinsic Parameters

The intrinsic parameters of each camera were calibrated prior to mounting using several positions of a planar 30×34 cm checkerboard target [1]. The intrinsic parameters of the PTZ cameras were calibrated at several different zoom levels, since the parameters vary during zooming. All the fixed camera as well as the dome PTZ camera were calibrated offline. The PTZ cameras are calibrated online.

Also, it can be seen that the radial distortion for fixed cameras are more serious than PTZ cameras even though they share the same focal length. This may be attributed to different characteristics of lens. Figure 5.2 shows a sample image before and after undistortion. The extrinsic parameters and re-projection error analysis of the calibration are shown in Fig. 5.3.

Fig. 5.2 Image before and after undistortion

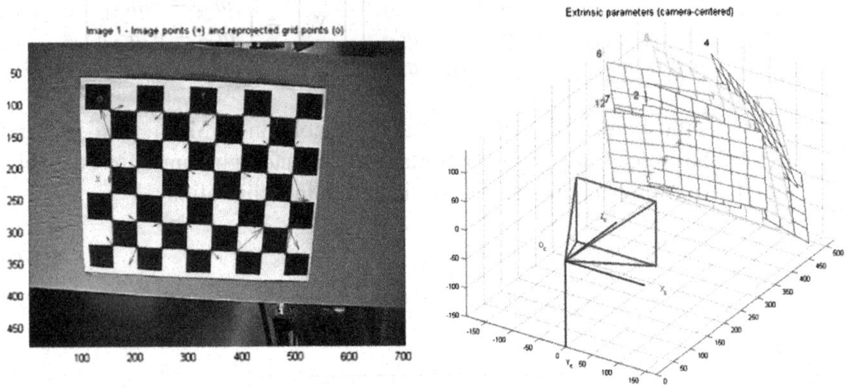

Fig. 5.3 Evaluation of calibration

5.4 Extrinsic Parameters Calibration

After calibrating the intrinsic parameters of the cameras, we need to know the relative position between each pair of cameras.

5.4.1 Calibrating Extrinsic Parameters with a Scale Bar

Let **E** be the essential matrix and **F** be the fundamental matrix of a stereo pair, we have

$$\mathbf{F} = \mathbf{K}_r^{-\top}\mathbf{E}\mathbf{K}_l^{-1} = \mathbf{K}_r^{-\top}\mathbf{R}[\mathbf{t}]_\times\mathbf{K}_l^{-1} \tag{5.9}$$

in which

$$[\mathbf{t}]_\times = \begin{bmatrix} 0 & -t_z & t_y \\ t_z & 0 & -t_x \\ -t_y & t_x & 0 \end{bmatrix}. \tag{5.10}$$

Let $\mathbf{p}_l$ and $\mathbf{p}_r$ be a pair of correspondence of a 3D point on the image planes of left and right camera, we have

$$\mathbf{p}_l^\top \mathbf{F}\mathbf{p}_r. \tag{5.11}$$

With more than eight pairs of correspondences, we can estimate $\mathbf{F}$ [3]. Then $\mathbf{E}$ can be obtained by

$$\mathbf{E} = \mathbf{K}_r^\top \mathbf{F}\mathbf{K}_l. \tag{5.12}$$

After applying *SVD* on $\mathbf{E}$, two possible rotation matrices $\mathbf{R}_1$ and $\mathbf{R}_2$, and a translation vector $\mathbf{t}'$ with an unknown scale factor can be obtained. Let $\mathbf{E} = \mathbf{U}\Lambda\mathbf{V}^\top$ after *SVD*, we have

$$\begin{cases} \mathbf{R}_1 = \mathbf{U}\mathbf{W}\mathbf{V}^\top \\ \mathbf{R}_2 = \mathbf{U}\mathbf{W}^\top\mathbf{V}^\top \\ \mathbf{t}' = \mathbf{U}\mathbf{Z}\mathbf{U}^\top \end{cases} \tag{5.13}$$

in which

$$\mathbf{W} = \begin{bmatrix} 0 & -1 & 0 \\ 1 & 0 & 0 \\ 0 & 0 & 1 \end{bmatrix}, \quad \mathbf{Z} = \begin{bmatrix} 0 & 1 & 0 \\ -1 & 0 & 0 \\ 0 & 0 & 0 \end{bmatrix}. \tag{5.14}$$

There are four choices for the extrinsic parameters, some criterions are given as following:

- Looking at which side of the cameras should a reconstructed 3D point lay. For most situations, the reconstructed 3D points should lay in front of the cameras (i.e., the reconstructed $z > 0$).
- The sign of $\mathbf{t}'$ can provide useful information in making the decision. For example, when the extrinsic parameters represent the transformation from left camera to right camera, t_x should be negative.

Since $\|\mathbf{t}'\| = 1$ and $\mathbf{t} = k\mathbf{t}'$, the scale factor k needs to be found in order to obtain translation vector $\mathbf{t}$. With a scale bar with two endpoints, distance L between which are well known, we can reconstruct the distance L' between them with the $\mathbf{R}$ and $\mathbf{t}'$ obtained before and find k by $k = \frac{L}{L'}$. Randomly place the scale bar in the FOV for n times, we can estimate the translation vector $\mathbf{t}$ by

$$\mathbf{t} = k\mathbf{t}' = \frac{L}{n}\sum_{i=1}^{n}\frac{1}{L_i'} \tag{5.15}$$

in which L_i' is the scale bar length estimated for the ith image.

5.4.2 Nonlinear Optimization

Error may be induced by noise on the images. Nonlinear optimization should be conducted on the calibration results with the previous linear results as initial estimations. First, let the scale bar length reconstructed for image i be L'_i, we can minimize the error between L'_i and L by

$$f_1(r_x, r_y, r_z, t_x, t_y, t_z) = \sum_{i=1}^{n} |L - L'_i| \tag{5.16}$$

in which $[r_x\ r_y\ r_z]^\top$ is the rotation vector obtained by applying Rodrigues' rotation formula on $\mathbf{R}$. Also, fundamental matrix $\mathbf{F}$ will not fit Eq. (5.11) well if there is error in the estimation of projection matrices. Let $\mathbf{p_l}^{ij}$ and $\mathbf{p_r}^{ij}$ be ith pair of correspondence on jth scale bar placement, we have a goal function as

$$f_2(r_x, r_y, r_z, t_x, t_y, t_z) = \sum_{i=1}^{n}\sum_{j=1}^{N} |\mathbf{p}_r^{ij\top}\mathbf{F}\mathbf{p}_l^{ij}| = \sum_{i=1}^{n}\sum_{j=1}^{N} |\mathbf{p}_r^{ij\top}\mathbf{K}_r^{-\top}\mathbf{R}[\mathbf{t}]_\times\mathbf{K}_l^{-1}\mathbf{p}_l^{ij}|. \tag{5.17}$$

Now we can conduct our first round of optimization on extrinsic parameters as

$$f_{ex}(\mathbf{x}) = \rho_1 f_1(\mathbf{x}) + \rho_2 f_2(\mathbf{x}) \tag{5.18}$$

in which

$$\mathbf{x} = [r_x\ r_y\ r_z\ t_x\ t_y\ t_z]$$

ρ_1 and ρ_2 are the importance factors for each part of minimization. In our case, we use $\rho_1 = 10,\ \rho_2 = 0.1$. The number o f unknown parameters is 6, but the target has to be placed at least 4 times because solving the fundamental matrix $\mathbf{F}$ needs at least 4 pairs of points. With the extrinsic parameters obtained by linear method above be the initial estimation, the optimized solution of the extrinsic parameters between the two cameras can be obtained by *Levenberg-Marquardt* Algorithm.

5.4.3 Global Optimization

The error of intrinsic parameters is affecting the estimation accuracy of extrinsic parameters. However, the error induced by focal length may be much more obvious than error of principal point and distortion coefficients, which may cause serious error in the calibration of extrinsic parameters and the measurement of stereo rig. We propose a combined global optimization method to include the intrinsic parameters in the bundle adjustment. We assume that the principal points are fixed for both of the cameras, now we have

$$\mathbf{x} = (r_x, r_y, r_z, t_x, t_y, t_z, f_x^l, f_y^l, f_x^r, f_y^r)$$

where (f_x^l, f_y^l) and (f_x^r, f_y^r) are the scale factors of left and right cameras respectively. Since

$$\begin{bmatrix} x/z \\ y/z \\ 1 \end{bmatrix} = \mathbf{K}_l^{-1} \begin{bmatrix} u_l \\ v_l \\ 1 \end{bmatrix} = \begin{bmatrix} r11\ r12\ r13 \\ r21\ r22\ r23 \\ r31\ r32\ r33 \end{bmatrix}^{-1} \mathbf{K}_r^{-1} \begin{bmatrix} u_r \\ v_r \\ 1 \end{bmatrix} \tag{5.19}$$

we have

$$\begin{aligned} &\frac{t_x - u_r t_z}{u_r(r_{31}u_l + r_{32}v_l + r_{33}) - (r_{11}u_l + r_{12}v_l + r_{13})} \\ &= \frac{t_y - v_r t_z}{v_r(r_{31}u_l + r_{32}v_l + r_{33}) - (r_{21}u_l + r_{22}v_l + r_{23})} \end{aligned} \tag{5.20}$$

we can set up a goal function minimizing

$$\begin{aligned} f_3(\mathbf{x}) = \sum_{i=1}^{n}\sum_{j=1}^{N} \Big\{ &(t_x - u_r^{ij} t_z) \left[v_r^{ij}(r_{31}u_l^{ij} + r_{32}v_l^{ij} + r_{33}) - (r_{21}u_l^{ij} + r_{22}v_l^{ij} + r_{23}) \right] \\ &-(t_y - v_r^{ij} t_z) \left[u_r^{ij}(r_{31}u_l^{ij} + r_{32}v_l^{ij} + r_{33}) - (r_{11}u_l^{ij} + r_{12}v_l^{ij} + r_{13}) \right] \Big\}. \end{aligned}$$

The new global minimization function becomes

$$f_g(\mathbf{x}) = \rho_1 f_1(\mathbf{x}) + \rho_2 f_2(\mathbf{x}) + \rho_3 f_3(\mathbf{x}). \tag{5.21}$$

The new minimization problem can be solved with *Levenberg-Marquardt* Algorithm resulting more accurate intrinsic and extrinsic parameters. This method is suitable for online calibration for camera network.

5.5 Feature Extraction

The features that need to be extracted are the centers of two active lighted balls on both ends of the scale bar. The length between the centers of the balls is 1181.10 mm. Regarding the complexity of background, for each position, two images of the scale bar should be taken by each camera with the lights on and off. Figure 5.4 shows sample image pairs for one position.

Fig. 5.4 Sample image pair for used in the calibration

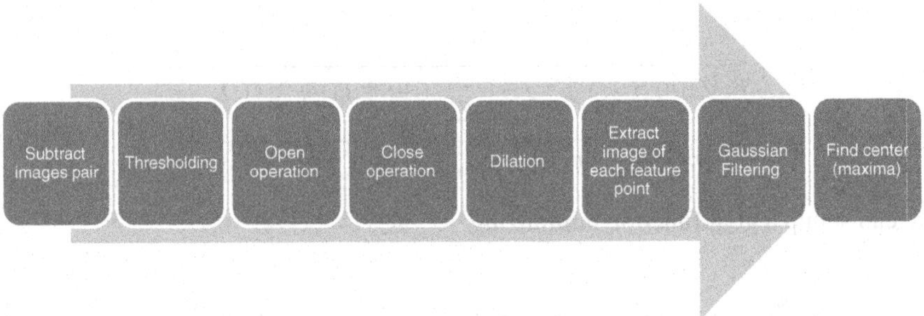

Fig. 5.5 Process for extracting the center of control points

The process of extracting the centers of control points are shown in Fig. 5.5. First, the image with lights on should be subtracted by the image with lights off, so that most of objects in the background can be removed. By applying thresholding and open operation, noise of small size or low level can be removed. However, these operations may cause small holes within the control point, which can be filled by applying close operation with disk-shaped structure element.

In order to precisely extract the center of the control point, gray scale image of each control point should be used. Dilate the result image obtained in previous step with disk-shaped structure element, and dot multiply it with original image with lights on, we can get images shown in Fig. 5.6a. It can be seen that the center of control point can be extracted by thresholding and finding the center of the connecting component. However, for better precision, a Gaussian filter can be applied on the image, the result image is shown in Fig. 5.6b. With which a sub-pixel level center of the control point can be found by finding the maxima by Hessian matrix.

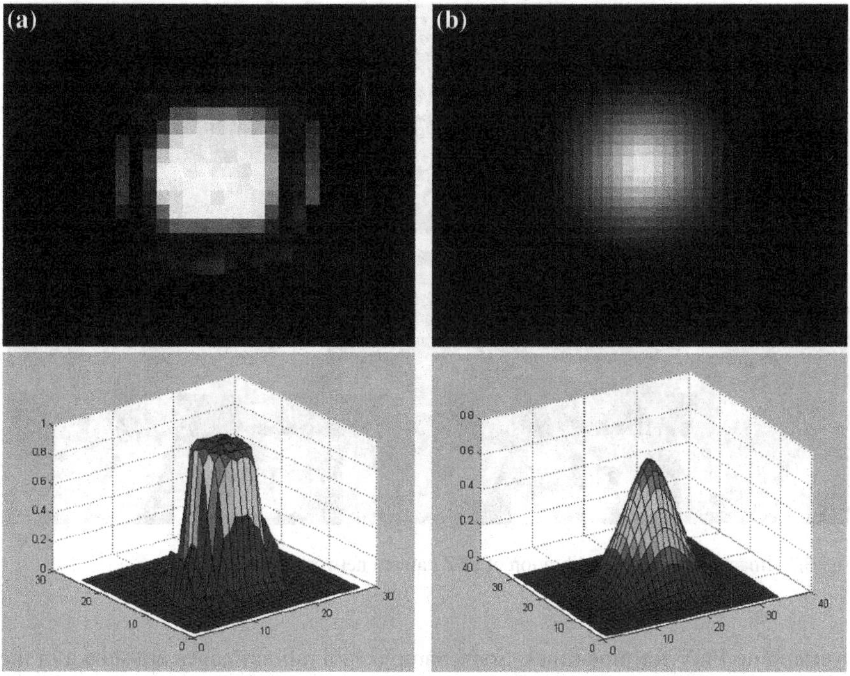

Fig. 5.6 Images of feature point before and after Gaussian filtering. **a** Original Image. **b** After Gaussian filter

5.6 Calibrating Pan-Tilt-Zoom Camera Network

We calibrated the PTZ cameras simultaneously, using a scale bar of known length (1.18 m) with two active lighting balls on its ends. First, we adjusted the pan and tilt parameters of the six PTZ cameras so that their fields of view overlapped. Then, we randomly placed the scale bar at 15–20 different noncoplanar positions, imaging the bar with both the room lights on and off. We extracted the centers of the actively lit balls in each on/off pair and used them as correspondences to estimate the essential matrix between each camera to be calibrated and the reference camera. Finally, we decomposed the essential matrices to obtain the extrinsic parameters (i.e., rotation matrix and translation vector) for each camera. Finally, we perform a bundle adjustment over the intrinsic and extrinsic parameters.

Three groups of calibration data in different positions are recorded. The position parameters of the cameras are shown in Fig. 5.6. Only one group of data are required for the shift between optical center and the rotation center of the PTZ cameras.

The effect and error induced by the shift will be discussed after future experiments and evaluation, and will be compensated/calibrated by more than two groups of calibration data. During the calibration, the scale bar was randomly placed in the

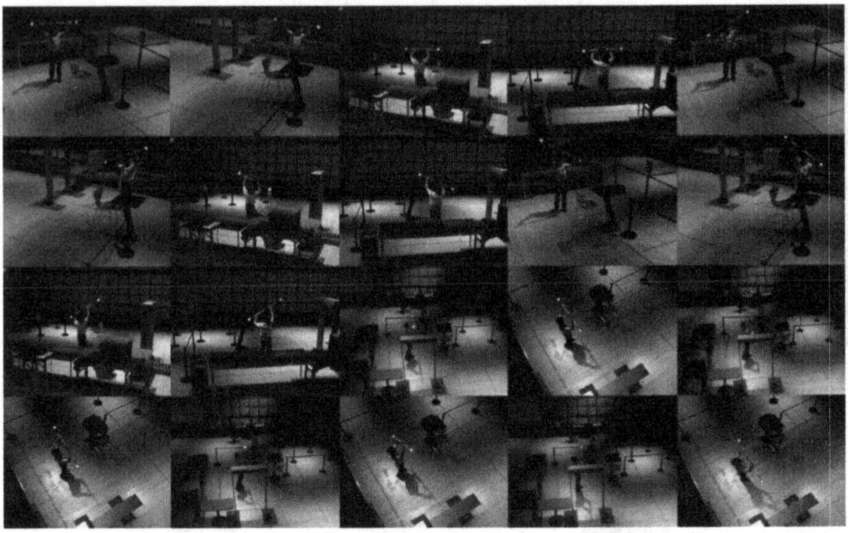

Fig. 5.7 Images used in the calibration of PTZ camera network

overlapping FOV for nine times. Some sample calibration images are shown in the Fig. 5.7.

After feature point extraction, we can get centers of control points of the scale bar for each camera in each position. Let the frame of camera 130 be the world frame, extrinsic parameter of each PTZ camera can be calibrated in pairs using the method in Sect. 5.4.

In order to evaluate the calibration results, the length of the scale bar is reconstructed for each image for every PTZ camera. However, measurement of the length of scale bar cannot reflect the precision of positioning of the stereo system. Since five PTZ cameras are calibrated at the same time, we have sufficient constraints to optimize the positioning performance of the system.

Let $\mathbf{P}_{ij}$ be a reconstructed feature point in 3D by camera i and camera j. In order to minimize the positioning error, defined as the difference between the reconstructed absolute coordinates of each feature point for every camera in the camera network, we have

$$\begin{aligned} f_d(\mathbf{x}) = & \, STD\left([\mathbf{P}_{12}\ \mathbf{P}_{13}\ \cdots\ \mathbf{P}_{1n}]\right) \\ & + STD\left([\mathbf{P}_{21}\ \mathbf{P}_{23}\ \cdots\ \mathbf{P}_{2n}]\right) \\ & + \cdots + STD\left(\left[\mathbf{P}_{n1}\ \mathbf{P}_{n2}\ \cdots\ \mathbf{P}_{n(n-1)}\right]\right) \end{aligned}$$

which can be added to the global optimization function (5.21) resulting:

$$f_g(\mathbf{x}) = \rho_1 f_1(\mathbf{x}) + \rho_2 f_2(\mathbf{x}) + \rho_3 f_3(\mathbf{x}) + \rho_4 f_d(\mathbf{x}). \qquad (5.22)$$

More precise positioning performance can be obtained by solving the new minimization function with *Levenberg-Marquardt* Algorithm. We observed a better performance of positioning achieved. However, the error of reconstructing the length of scale bar may slightly increase.

5.7 Calibrating Fixed Camera Network

Next, we calibrated the fixed cameras using the PTZ cameras as reference. Each fixed camera was calibrated with respect to the closest PTZ camera, changing the pan and tilt of this camera to obtain the best image overlap. As before, the scale bar was imaged in different positions to obtain feature points, and the essential matrix decomposed to obtain the extrinsic parameters. Finally, since each fixed camera was calibrated with respect to a different reference, the results are unified to a common coordinate system by a series of appropriate rotations and translations.

After finding the relation between PTZ camera and the fixed cameras to be calibrated using the method mentioned in Sect. 5.4, a pure rotation matrix should be applied in order to unify the fixed camera to the world frame. Let the direction of rotation be as follows: $\mathbf{R}_x$ rotates the y-axis towards the z-axis, $\mathbf{R}_y$ rotates the z-axis towards the x-axis, and $\mathbf{R}_z$ rotates the x-axis towards the y-axis, the final rotation matrix for PTZ camera pure rotation is

$$\mathbf{R}_p = \mathbf{R}_x(\theta)\mathbf{R}_y(\phi)\mathbf{R}_z(\varphi) \tag{5.23}$$

in which

$$\mathbf{R}_x(\theta) = \begin{bmatrix} 1 & 0 & 0 \\ 0 & \cos\theta & -\sin\theta \\ 0 & \sin\theta & \cos\theta \end{bmatrix} \tag{5.24}$$

$$\mathbf{R}_y(\phi) = \begin{bmatrix} \cos\phi & 0 & \sin\phi \\ 0 & 1 & 0 \\ -\sin\phi & 0 & \cos\phi \end{bmatrix} \tag{5.25}$$

$$\mathbf{R}_z(\varphi) = \begin{bmatrix} \cos\varphi & -\sin\varphi & 0 \\ \sin\varphi & \cos\varphi & 0 \\ 0 & 0 & 1 \end{bmatrix}. \tag{5.26}$$

Let $[\mathbf{R}_{WCi}\ \mathbf{T}_{WCi}]$ be the extrinsic parameters of Camera i in the world frame, $[\mathbf{R}_{PCi}\ \mathbf{T}_{PCi}]$ be the extrinsic parameters between PTZ camera and Camera i, and $[\mathbf{R}_{WP}\ \mathbf{T}_{WP}]$ be the extrinsic parameters of PTZ camera in the world frame, we have:

$$\begin{cases} \mathbf{R}_{WCi} = \mathbf{R}_{PCi}\mathbf{R}_P\mathbf{R}_{WP} \\ \mathbf{T}_{WCi} = \mathbf{R}_{PCi}\mathbf{R}_P\mathbf{T}_{WP} + \mathbf{T}_{PCi} \end{cases}. \tag{5.27}$$

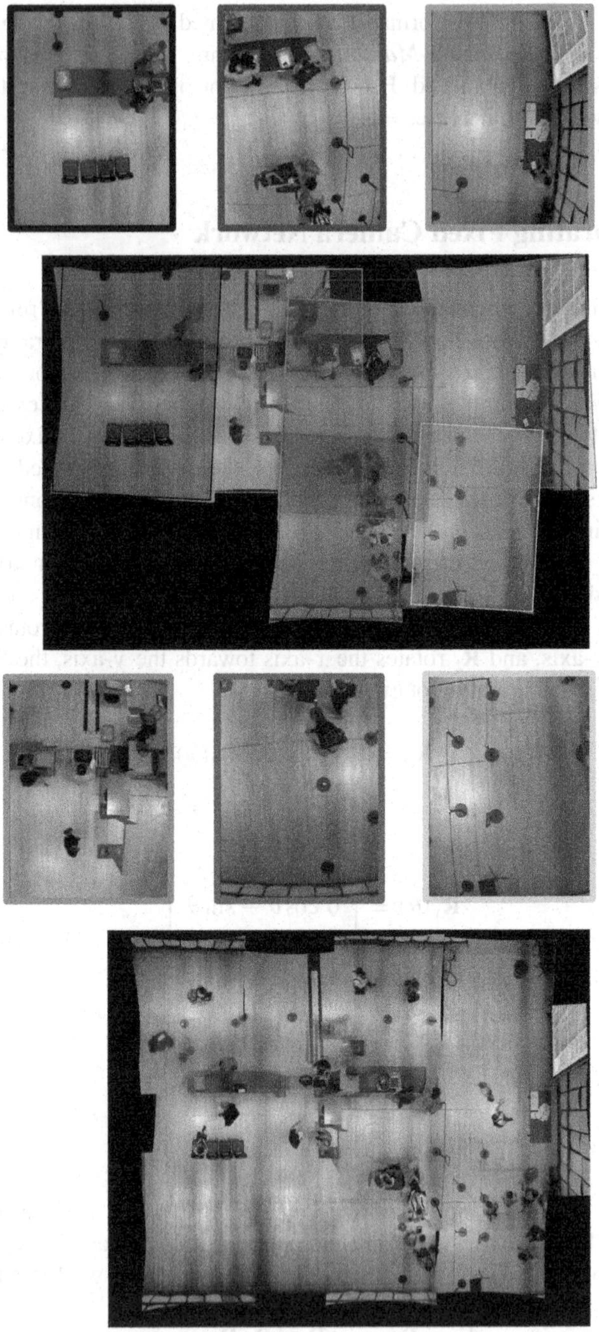

Fig. 5.8 Stitched images using a subset of the cameras and the calibration results

Same method as calibrating PTZ cameras is used to evaluate the calibration precision of fixed cameras. The errors in measuring length of scale bar range from 1–4 mm, while the percentage errors range from 0.1–0.3 %. Further global optimization may be applied in future experiments. Figure 5.8 shows an example stitched images using six cameras and their calibration results.

5.8 Discussion

The camera network consisting multiple cameras are presented and calibrated. A scale bar with two control points is used in the extrinsic calibration. Due to limitation of overlapping area between fixed cameras, PTZ cameras are first calibrated simultaneously. By including intrinsic parameters in the bundle adjustment, the calibration precision is improved and the convergence speed is reduced. Then, the positioning precision of the stereo system is improved by adding the constraint of minimizing the difference between feature points coordinates reconstructed by different combination of PTZ cameras in pairs during the optimization. After that, the fixed cameras are calibrated with two of the calibrated PTZ cameras and then unified to the world frame. The error induced by the shift between the optical center and the rotation center of PTZ cameras are remaining to be calibrated in future experiments.

References

1. Z. Zhang, A flexible new technique for camera calibration. IEEE Trans. Pattern Anal. Mach. Intell. **22**, 1330–1334 (2000)
2. Z. Zhang, Q. Luong, O. Faugeras, Motion of an uncalibrated stereo rig: self-calibration and metric reconstruction. IEEE Trans. Robot. Autom. **12**, 103–113 (1996)
3. R. Hartley, In defense of the eight-point algorithm. IEEE Trans. Pattern Anal. Mach. Intell. **19**, 580–593 (1997)
4. D. Devarajan, R. Radke, Calibrating distributed camera networks. Proc. IEEE **96**, 1625–1639 (2008)
5. S. Sinha, M. Pollefeys, Synchronization and calibration of camera networks from silhouettes. Proc. 17th Int. Conf. Pattern Recognit. **1**, 116–119 (2004)
6. Rahimi, A. Rahimi, B. Dunagan, T. Darrell, Simultaneous calibration and tracking with a network of non-overlapping sensors, in *Proceedings of the IEEE Conference Computer Vision and Pattern Recognition* (2004), pp. 187–194

Part III
Core Analytic for Human Re-Identification

In the last part of the book, novel core analytic algorithms for human re-identification problem are presented, including feature extraction, signature building, off-line metric learning, and online unsupervised learning.

Chapter 6
Learning Viewpoint Invariant Signatures

When it comes to recognizing and matching the identity of a person, finger prints and face are considered the most representative and discriminative from the perspective of biometrics, which are also considered as the 'signatures' of a person. In person re-identification community, Although features and representations have been studied extensively for human re-identification, most of them only works under strong assumptions such as ignoring perspective distortion or difference in camera viewpoints. Although these representations shows promising results on benchmark datasets, they are likely to fail in real-world scenarios.

For instance, surveillance cameras are usually mounted on the ceiling to avoid clutters and occlusion, which can cause serious perspective distortion. In contrast, most of the mainstream human re-identification benchmark datasets come with images taken with a camera from viewpoints perpendicular to the ground plane, which is obviously different from the actual case in real-world re-identification applications (i.e., large angles, $\sim$45–90°).

Most of the popular representations [1–9] currently being used in human re-identification studies, tend to divide the sub-image (i.e., cropped image containing mostly just the person) into patches or vertical stripes [1]. Apparently, consistent performance cannot be expected using this signature in matching two images taken from different camera viewpoint. In this chapter, we are going to introduce approaches and algorithms necessary to obtain signatures that are independent from camera viewpoints.

6.1 Eliminating Perspective Distortion

Perspective distortion refers to image distortion due to perspective transform, specifically when the incident angle of the camera optical axis with respect to the normal of floor plane is small, as illustrated in Fig. 6.1.

Z. Wu, *Human Re-Identification*, Multimedia Systems and Applications,
DOI 10.1007/978-3-319-40991-7_6

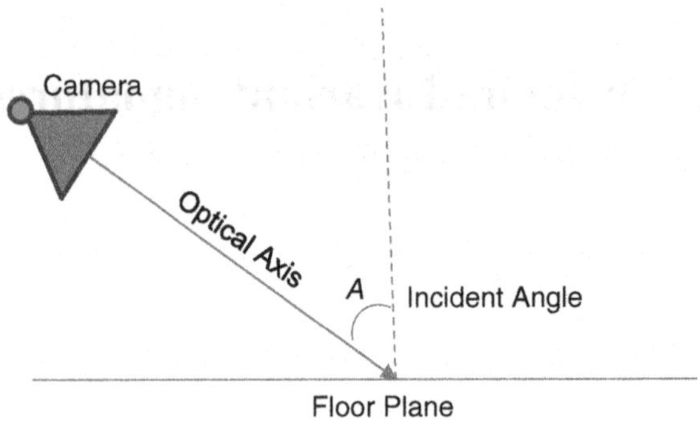

Fig. 6.1 Illustration incident angle

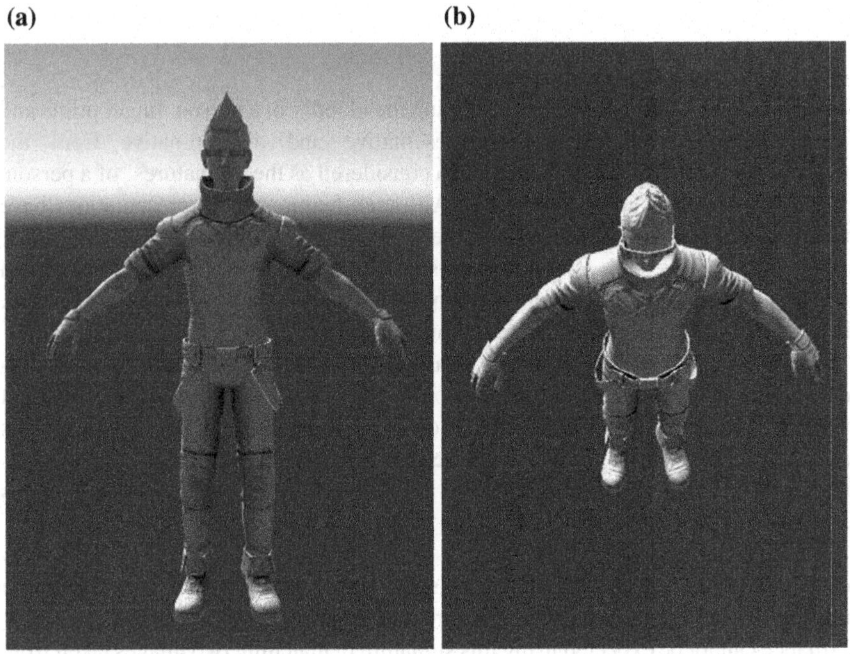

Fig. 6.2 Looking at people from different viewpoint. **a** Viewpoint A. **b** Viewpoint B

A simple example can be found in Fig. 6.2, where sub-figure (a) is an image taken with large incident angle viewpoint while sub-figure (b) is an image taken with small incident angle viewpoint.

In order to eliminate the perspective distortion, i.e., recover the ratio of the body parts for the person in the sub-image, as if the camera viewpoint is perpendicular to the normal direction of the floor plane, a process named "rectification" needs to be done [10–12].

First, the camera needs to be calibrated w.r.t. to the floor plane. This can be done by placing markers with known distances on the floor (i.e., control points), or using the parallel lines and objects under tracking [13]. Even by simply labeling or tracking the trajectories of moving objects on the floor plane in the view, the accuracy of calibration should be accurate enough for the purpose of rectification.

Let the floor plane coincides with the $X-Y$ plane of the world coordinate system. For a 3D point $\tilde{\mathbf{Z}} = \mathbf{z} = \begin{bmatrix} x \\ y \\ z \end{bmatrix}$, we have

$$\lambda \mathbf{z} = \mathbf{K} \begin{bmatrix} \mathbf{R} & \mathbf{t} \\ \mathbf{0} & 1 \end{bmatrix} \tilde{\mathbf{Z}} \tag{6.1}$$

where

$$\mathbf{z} = \begin{bmatrix} u \\ v \end{bmatrix}$$

is the homogeneous coordinate of the corresponding projected 2D point on the image plane,

$$\mathbf{K} = \begin{bmatrix} f_x & 0 & c_x \\ 0 & f_y & c_y \\ 0 & 0 & 1 \end{bmatrix}$$

is the intrinsic parameter obtained from the camera calibration. $\mathbf{R}$ and $\mathbf{t}$ are the rotation matrix and translation vector respectively, representing the transformation from the world coordinate system to the camera coordinate system, where

$$\mathbf{R} = \begin{bmatrix} r_{11} & r_{12} & r_{13} \\ r_{21} & r_{22} & r_{23} \\ r_{31} & r_{32} & r_{33} \end{bmatrix}$$

and

$$\mathbf{t} = \begin{bmatrix} t_1 \\ t_2 \\ t_3 \end{bmatrix}$$

When only considering 3D points on the $X-Y$ plane in the world coordinate system, the z element of $\tilde{\mathbf{Z}}$ is always zero. Hence Eq. (6.1) becomes

$$\lambda \mathbf{z} = \mathbf{K} \begin{bmatrix} r_{11} & r_{12} & t_1 \\ r_{21} & r_{22} & t_2 \\ r_{31} & r_{32} & t_3 \end{bmatrix} \begin{bmatrix} x \\ y \\ 1 \end{bmatrix} = \mathbf{H} \begin{bmatrix} x \\ y \\ 1 \end{bmatrix} = \mathbf{H}\tilde{\mathbf{Z}}' \tag{6.2}$$

Here $\mathbf{H}$ is the homography matrix between the camera image plane and the $X-Y$ floor plane, which can be obtained by annotating more than four pairs of corresponding points on the floor plane and image plane (i.e., full calibration of the camera is actually not required, but is recommended for better accuracy).

Once we have the $\mathbf{H}$, the 3D location $\tilde{\mathbf{Z}}_\mathbf{f} = \begin{bmatrix} x_f \\ y_f \\ 1 \end{bmatrix}$ of the feet of the person under tracking on the floor can be recovered from their 2D projection on the image plane $\mathbf{z_f} = \begin{bmatrix} u_f \\ v_f \\ 1 \end{bmatrix}$ by:

$$\tilde{\mathbf{Z}}_\mathbf{f} \sim \mathbf{H}^{-1}\mathbf{z_f} \tag{6.3}$$

Given an estimation of the height h of the person, the 3D position of the head $\tilde{\mathbf{Z}}_\mathbf{h} = \begin{bmatrix} x_f \\ y_f \\ h \end{bmatrix}$ will also be required to in order to establish correspondence to the head position in the image. Let $\mathbf{z_h} = \begin{bmatrix} u_h \\ v_h \\ 1 \end{bmatrix}$ be the projection of the head position on the image plane, we have

$$h\mathbf{m_3} = \mathbf{z_h} - \begin{bmatrix} \mathbf{m_1} & \mathbf{m_2} & \mathbf{m_4} \end{bmatrix}^\top \tilde{\mathbf{Z}}_\mathbf{h} \tag{6.4}$$

where $\mathbf{m_i}$ is the ith column of $\mathbf{M} = \mathbf{K}[\mathbf{R}|\mathbf{t}]$.

With $\tilde{\mathbf{Z}}_\mathbf{h}$ and $\tilde{\mathbf{Z}}_\mathbf{f}$, a 3D cylinder orthogonal to the ground plane with height h and radius w can be inferred. Here w can either be computed by the width of the sub-image, i.e., the width of the bounding box when detecting the person, or a fixed value. The horizontal cylindrical segment with normal direction parallel to the line between $\tilde{\mathbf{Z}}_\mathbf{f}$ and the projection of the camera optical center on the floor plane would be our desired frontal, perspective-distortion-free bounding box, noted as $\overline{\mathbf{N_aN_bN_cN_d}}$. Now the next step would be finding the corresponding projections of this horizontal cylindrical segment on the camera image plane, defined as polygon $\overline{\mathbf{n_an_bn_cn_d}}$.

Let $\mathbf{C}$ be the 3D location of the camera and $\mathbf{Z_c}$ be the projection of $\mathbf{C}$ on the $X-Y$ plane (floor plane). The rectified sub-image of the detected target can then be obtained. Let the projection of $\overline{\mathbf{CZ_f}}$ onto the ground plane be $\overline{\mathbf{Z_cZ_f}}$. The rectified sub-image $\overline{\mathbf{N_aN_bN_cN_d}}$ is parallel to the Z axis and orthogonal to $\overline{\mathbf{Z_cZ_f}}$. Hence the desired 3D points in Fig. 6.3 can then be found as

Fig. 6.3 Illustration of sub-image rectification

$$N_a = \begin{bmatrix} x_f + w\cos\left(\arctan\left(\frac{x_c - x_f}{y_c - y_f}\right)\right) \\ y_f + w\sin\left(\arctan\left(\frac{x_c - x_f}{y_c - y_f}\right)\right) \\ 0 \end{bmatrix}$$

$$N_b = \begin{bmatrix} x_f - w\cos\left(\arctan\left(\frac{x_c - x_f}{y_c - y_f}\right)\right) \\ y_f - w\sin\left(\arctan\left(\frac{x_c - x_f}{y_c - y_f}\right)\right) \\ 0 \end{bmatrix}$$

$$N_c = \begin{bmatrix} x_f + w\cos\left(\arctan\left(\frac{x_c - x_f}{y_c - y_f}\right)\right) \\ y_f + w\sin\left(\arctan\left(\frac{x_c - x_f}{y_c - y_f}\right)\right) \\ h \end{bmatrix}$$

$$N_d = \begin{bmatrix} x_f - w\cos\left(\arctan\left(\frac{x_c - x_f}{y_c - y_f}\right)\right) \\ y_f - w\sin\left(\arctan\left(\frac{x_c - x_f}{y_c - y_f}\right)\right) \\ h \end{bmatrix}.$$

Now we have the correspondences, the homography between the 3D horizontal cylindrical segment and the polygon on the image plane defined by $\overline{\mathbf{n_a n_b n_c n_d}}$ and $\overline{\mathbf{N_a N_b N_c N_d}}$ respectively can then be computed and used to create a new rectified image in which the person appears to be vertical, and perspective-distortion-free, as illustrated in Figs. 6.3 and 6.4.

As the person moves between two points on the floor, we obtain two 3D positions $\tilde{\mathbf{Z}}_{\mathbf{f}_1}$ and $\tilde{\mathbf{Z}}_{\mathbf{f}_2}$. The viewpoint angle of the person with respect to the camera can be estimated by

$$\theta = \arccos\left(\frac{(\tilde{\mathbf{Z}}_{\mathbf{f}_2} - \tilde{\mathbf{Z}}_{\mathbf{f}_1})^\top (\mathbf{Z}_c - \tilde{\mathbf{Z}}_{\mathbf{f}_1})}{\|\tilde{\mathbf{Z}}_{\mathbf{f}_2} - \tilde{\mathbf{Z}}_{\mathbf{f}_1}\| \|\mathbf{Z}_c - \tilde{\mathbf{Z}}_{\mathbf{f}_1}\|}\right). \tag{6.5}$$

We will talk about making use of this viewpoint angle to learn the viewpoint invariant representation in following sections.

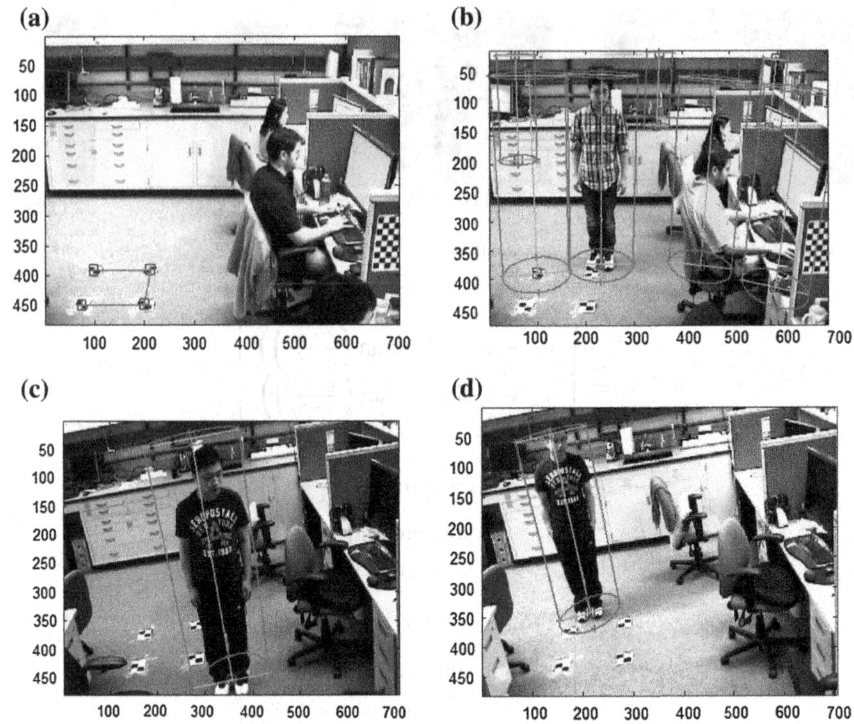

Fig. 6.4 **a** Marked features on the floor used in the calibration. **b–d** Estimated cylinders containing targets at different locations

6.2 Learning Signatures with Pose Prior

Figure 6.5 shows a few examples of image pairs selected from the VIPeR dataset [1] and the i-Lids dataset [14]. While the readers can easily tell the fact that each image pair in the figure consist of two images taken from two cameras looking at the person from different viewpoints, it is not as easy for our classifiers. For example, the handbag of the woman in red would not be visible if the camera is frontal viewing while it is very obvious when looking from the side direction. If we treat these two images equally, error will be induced in extracting signatures.

So we know, looking at a person from different viewpoint shall expect different features. This is not a bad thing, but when it comes to human re-identification, we want the signatures we extract to be discriminative, that is, we should be able to obtain very similar features from any viewpoint.

In the previous chapter, while rectifying the sub-images, we obtained the viewpoint angle of the camera with respect to the person. Let us take one of the strip-based feature extraction method as an example [1]; sub-image of a human is divided into horizontal strips, in which color and texture features are extracted and

(a) **(b)**

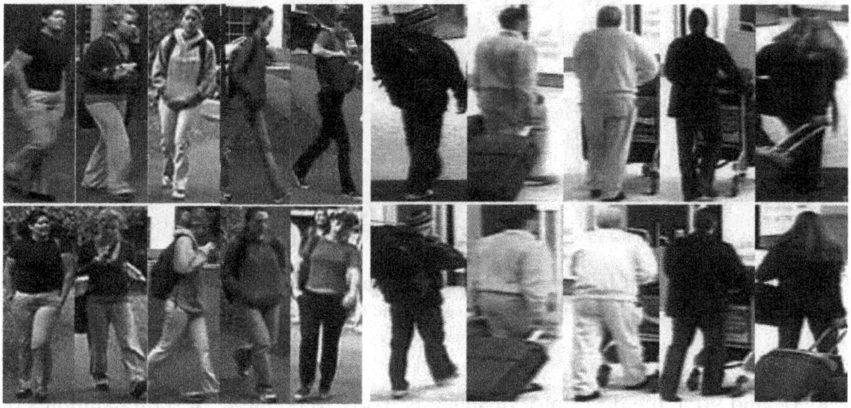

Fig. 6.5 **a** Sample images from the VIPeR dataset [1]. **b** Sample images from the i-Lids dataset [14]

concatenated into a feature vector $\mathbf{X}$. Let $\mathbf{X}_a$ and $\mathbf{X}_b$ be two descriptors extracted from two sub-images, essentially the human re-identification is to determine if these two sub-images belong to the same person, based on the distance between $\mathbf{X}_a$ and $\mathbf{X}_b$, that is

$$y = f(\mathbf{X}_a, \mathbf{X}_b) \tag{6.6}$$

where $f(x)$ is the distance function, e.g. Euclidean distance, Mahalanobis distance, L1 Norm, or L2 Norm. These distance functions can be applied on the fly without any prior knowledge or data about the deployment environment and infrastructures, etc. However in the case that we have the data, and want to adapt to the environment, learning-based distance metrics are used, where

$$f(\mathbf{X}_a, \mathbf{X}_b) = \mathbf{W}^\top |\mathbf{X}_a - \mathbf{X}_b| \tag{6.7}$$

where $\mathbf{W}^\top$ is the learned distance metric, in the form of a vector. One can consider the numbers in the vector to be the "weights" of the corresponding features in $\mathbf{X}_a$ and $\mathbf{X}_b$. Features with higher weights are considered more "discriminative" while features with lower weights are either common (i.e., can be found on everyone), or unstable (e.g., noise or incidental).

Distance metric $\mathbf{W}^\top$ is entirely trained with training data. The motivation behind extracting feature histograms over horizontal strips [1] is to make the feature extraction invariant to rotation around the major axis direction (i.e., the direction from feet to top of head) of human to some extent. However this only works when the difference in viewpoint between $\mathbf{X}_a$ and $\mathbf{X}_b$ is small enough. Figure 6.6 shows a few examples.

While this approach is reasonable with images taken from the same point of view, when matching a pair of images of the same person from different viewpoints

Fig. 6.6 Example image pairs that may cause serious matching errors if the same descriptor is used without regard to pose. The *yellow rectangles* show the most difficult parts

(e.g., 0° and 90°), the descriptor distance is likely to be large. Several examples of this problem are shown in Fig. 6.6.

As it can be seen in the figure, when viewpoint difference is relatively large (e.g., 0° and 90°), content in the same horizontal strips can be very distinct. Let us take a step back and think about this—Can we encapsulate the viewpoint information θ in the process of feature extraction?

Suppose we can model the signature $\mathbf{X}$ as a function of the human pose i.e.,

$$\mathbf{X} = X(\mathbf{I}, \theta) \tag{6.8}$$

We call (6.8) the "Pose Prior" [15], where $\mathbf{I}$ is the sub-image, and θ is the pose/viewpoint of the person in the sub-image. Equation (6.7) becomes

$$f(\mathbf{I}_a, \mathbf{I}_b) = \mathbf{W}^\top |X(\mathbf{I}_a, \theta_a) - X(\mathbf{I}_b, \theta_b)| \tag{6.9}$$

in which $\mathbf{I}_a$ and $\mathbf{I}_b$ are the sub-images after rectification to be matched, θ_a and θ_b are the poses of the person in the images respectively. $X(\mathbf{I}_a, \theta_a)$ and $X(\mathbf{I}_b, \theta_b)$ are the signatures extracted with pose prior. In other words, in the case of $\mathbf{I}_a$ and $\mathbf{I}_b$ are images of the same person, $|X(\mathbf{I}_a, \theta_a) - X(\mathbf{I}_b, \theta_b)|$ should be very small, independent of the viewpoint differences between θ_a and θ_b.

6.2.1 Learning Pose Prior

In order to learn viewpoint invariant signatures, we define our pose prior as, the prior information indicating the relationship between feature stability and the spatial location of each pixel, given viewpoint information.

Figure 6.7 shows a few examples of images of a person with different poses/camera viewpoints. It can be seen that, e.g., if a person is wearing a bag, central strips viewpoints in the range of 90°–180° are usually unreliable. Similar observation can

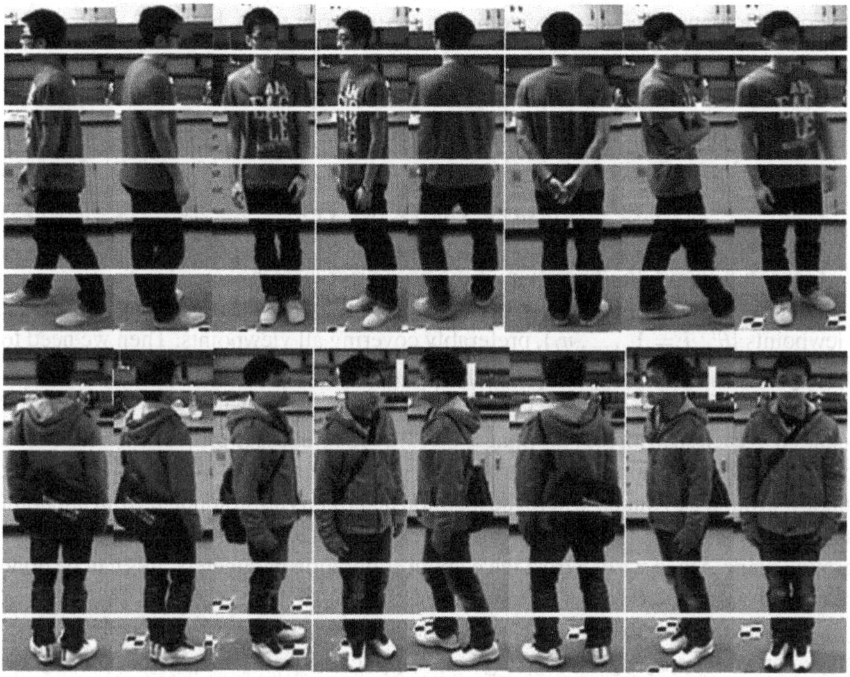

Fig. 6.7 Example images of person looking from different viewpoints

be found on the top strips where head can be seen. When looking from 180°, features extracted could be less meaningful.

First, we need to define a reference viewpoint, for example, when $\theta = 0$. Let the number of strips on a single sub-image be 6, we have

$$\mathbf{X}_F = \{\mathbf{x}_F^1, \ldots, \mathbf{x}_F^6\} \tag{6.10}$$

where $\mathbf{x}_F^k$ is the feature vector from the kth strip in the sub-image taken from frontal viewpoint ($\theta = 0$). We define a patch centered at column location u from strip k to be

$$\mathbf{I}^k(u) = \{\mathbf{I}(x, y) | u - w_h \leq x \leq u + w_h, u - w_v \leq y \leq u + w_v\} \tag{6.11}$$

where $\mathbf{I}(x, y)$ is a pixel at the location of (x, y) on the image, w_h is the width of the path and w_v is the height of a strip. In order to evaluate how similar is an image taken from another viewpoint θ, we extract the feature vector $\mathbf{x}^k(u)$ from $\mathbf{I}^k(u)$ and compare to the reference signature from the same strip (from viewpoint $\theta = 0$), i.e., $\mathbf{X}_F^k$. Note that here $\mathbf{X}_F$ is the signature on the full strip. Also coarse background subtraction is recommended.

For each feature vector $\mathbf{x}$, we compute its similarity to $\mathbf{X}_F$ by

$$p = \mathrm{Corr}(\mathbf{x}, \mathbf{X}_F) \tag{6.12}$$

With u spanning the whole strip, we can learn a function of the similarity as

$$p^k(u) = \mathrm{Corr}(\mathbf{x}^k(u), \mathbf{x}_F^k). \tag{6.13}$$

Figure 6.8 shows an illustration of the pose prior learning.

For a subject i, we compute $p^k(u)$ for each strip for images captured from several viewpoints $\{\theta_j^i, j = 1, \ldots, n_i\}$, preferably covering all viewpoints. Then we need to aggregate the individual pose priors $p^k(u)$ into a continue function $P(\theta)$, where θ is the viewpoint angle and $P(\theta)$ is a 2D matrix containing weights for each column location in each strip on the sub-image. One way to do this is to project these functions onto a circle by wrapping the correlation score function $p^k(u)$ at each viewpoint angle θ around a cylinder, where the location and radius are computed from apparent size of the person in the sub-image since normally the person is orthogonal to the ground plane. Since we can trust the camera calibration parameters, this can be done reasonably accurate (Fig. 6.9).

With N training subjects, we can accumulate the each pose prior measure together since here we are trying to learn a general applicable prior independent of subjects at each viewpoint angle θ we determine $P(\theta)$ by

$$P(\theta) = \mathrm{Mode}\,(P_1(\theta), \ldots, P_N(\theta)) \tag{6.14}$$

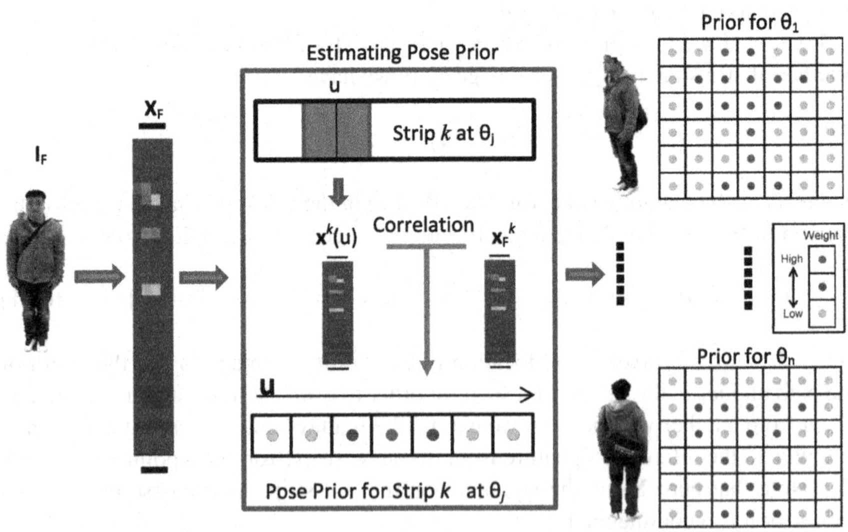

Fig. 6.8 Learning the pose prior

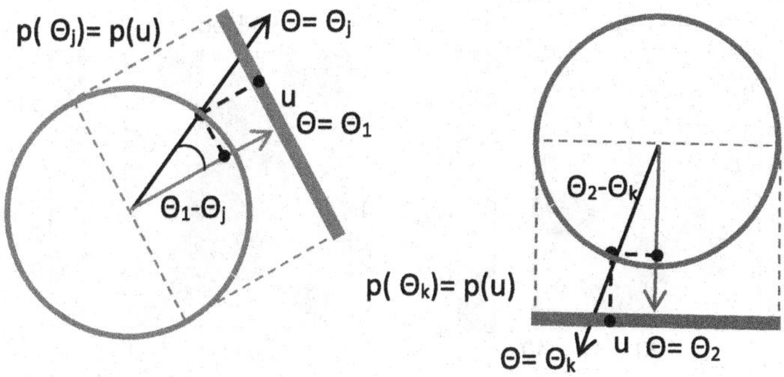

Fig. 6.9 Complete pose prior generated by projections of pose priors calculated from multiple viewpoints

where $P_1(\theta), \ldots, P_N(\theta)$ are all measurements corresponding to viewpoint θ. At this point, coarse background subtraction is assumed to be done and the foreground should be stretched horizontally to fill the sub-image for better accuracy. In the case that multiple modes exist, select the mode that corresponds to smaller value (weight) since multiple-mode indicates unreliable features.

Algorithm 1 shows the overall algorithm in learning pose prior.

Algorithm 1: Learning pose prior for accurate feature extraction.

Input: N: the number of people in training dataset
$\{n_1, \ldots, n_N\}$: the number of instances for a person
$\mathbf{I}_{Fi}$:Frontal view, $i = 1...N$
$\mathbf{I}_{\theta_j^i}$, $j = 1, \ldots, n_i$: Image of person i with viewpoint θ_j
Output: The learned pose prior $P(\theta)$
for $i = 1$ ***to*** N **do**
  Extract descriptors X_F^i for $\mathbf{I}_F^i$;
  for $j = 1$ ***to*** n_i **do**
    | Find $p_i(\theta_j^i)$ with Eq. (6.13);
  end
  for $\theta = 1$ ***to*** 360 **do**
    | Find $P_i(\theta)$ as $p_i(\theta_j^i) = \arg\min |\theta - \theta_j^i|$;
  end
end
for $\theta = 1$ ***to*** 360 **do**
  | Find $P(\theta)$ with Eq. (6.14);
end

Figure 6.10 shows examples of the trained pose prior at 45, 90, 135 and 180 degrees.

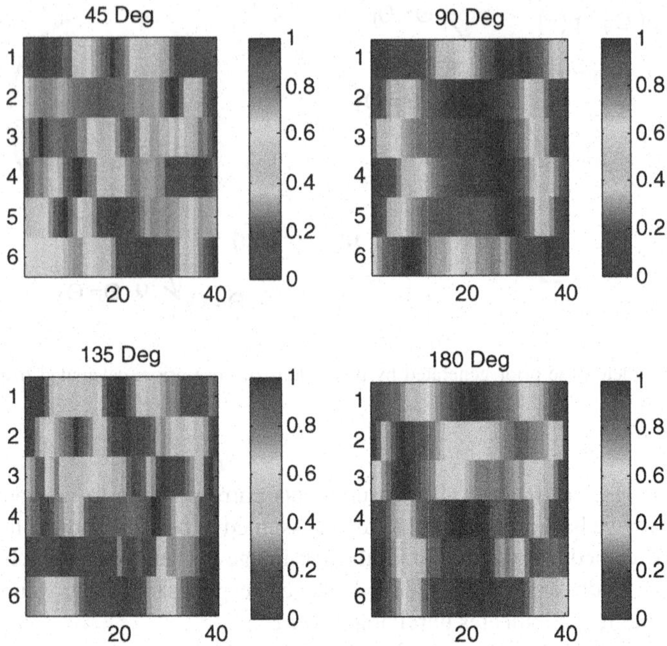

Fig. 6.10 Examples of the trained pose prior. It can be seen that the results match our assumptions. For example, at 90 degrees, the weights on the *right side* are much heavier than on the *left side*. At 135 and 180 degrees, the weights in the central area (i.e., the back of the person) are significantly lower than the neighboring areas. We found this phenomenon to be generally caused by people wearing backpacks

6.3 Learning Distance Metric with Pose Prior

Now we have the viewpoint invariant features with pose prior, the signatures become reliable and robust. Since we have the training data, we can also learn a discriminative distance metric [16, 17] for matching the signatures. Learning a distance metric is like an adaptation process for both the targets and the environment.

Once we learned the viewpoint invariant signatures with pose prior $P(\theta)$, we produce signatures by first extracting the raw features vectors before weighting the contributions of each column from each strip in calculating the histograms for each feature channel

$$\mathbf{x}_j^k(i) = \sum_{\substack{(u,v)\in \text{strip } k \\ \text{feature } j \text{ at } (u,v)\in \text{bin } i}} P_u^k(\theta) \tag{6.15}$$

where θ is the viewpoint angle, $\mathbf{x}_j^k(i)$ is the feature vector weighted with pose prior for strip k, $P_u^k(\theta)$ is the pose prior for stripe k at column u. That is, in calculating the value for each bin in the histogram of a particular feature channel, instead of considering binary result $\{0, 1\}$ from each pixel, it is actually weighting the result

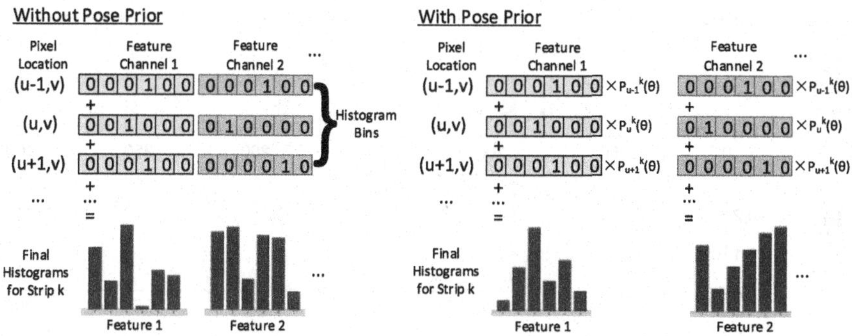

Fig. 6.11 The illustration of the difference between building descriptors with and without pose prior

by the pose prior $P_u^k(\theta)$. In other words, the contribution towards a bin becomes $\{0, P_u^k(\theta)\}$.

Since the descriptor entries are the counts in the bins of a histogram, in the absence of the pose prior, a feature value falling in bin i would increment the corresponding descriptor vector element by 1. With the pose prior, a feature value falling in bin i would increment the corresponding descriptor vector element by $P_u^k(\theta) \in [0, 1]$. Figure 6.11 below illustrates how the descriptor is computed with and without the pose prior.

Then conventional metric learning approaches can be applied (e.g., [18]). Given the constraints that, let

$$\mathbf{d}_{\text{same}} = |\mathbf{d}_\mathbf{j}^\mathbf{i} - \mathbf{d}_\mathbf{k}^\mathbf{i}| \tag{6.16}$$

be the absolute distance of two signatures belonging to the same person, and

$$\mathbf{d}_{\text{diff}} = |\mathbf{d}_\mathbf{j}^\mathbf{i} - \mathbf{d}_\mathbf{k}^\mathbf{l}| \tag{6.17}$$

be the absolute distance of two signatures belonging to different persons i and j, we require

$$\mathbf{W}^\top \mathbf{d}_{\text{same}} < \mathbf{W}^\top \mathbf{d}_{\text{diff}} \tag{6.18}$$

for any possible signature pairs from the training sample set.

An example can be found in Fig. 6.12 where, without pose prior the distance between two sub-image of the same person is large when viewing from different angle. After applying pose prior in calculating the signatures, the distance of the same image pair has been reduced significantly, suggesting that pose prior can effectively reduce the intra-class distance for human re-identification problem. Note that, here the absolute distance of the signatures is used since previous studies [2] have shown that more consistent and stable distance measure can be obtained with absolute distance.

Figure 6.13 shows two examples of improved ranking result brought by pose prior. In the example on top, the ground truth match lies in rank 10. With the help of pose

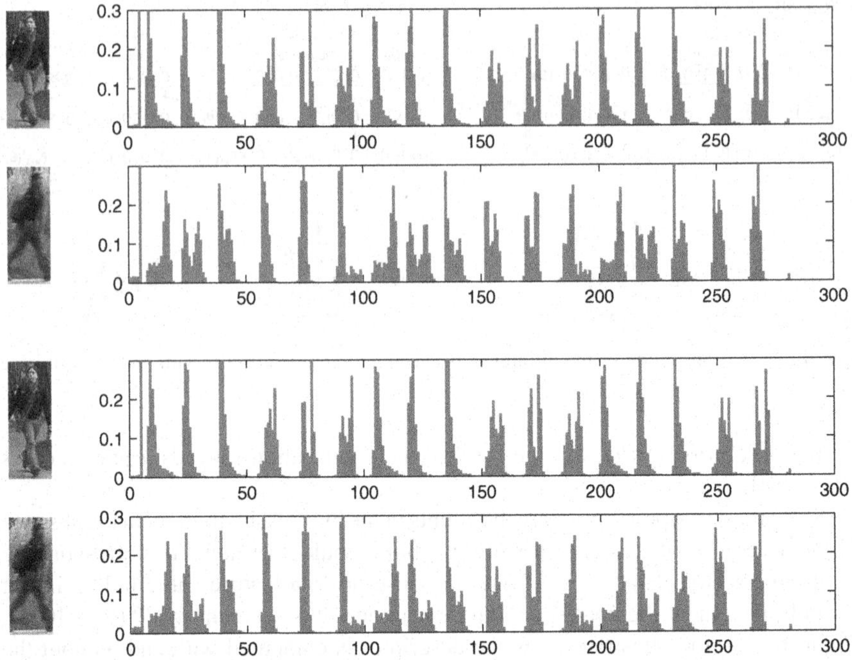

Fig. 6.12 The distance between descriptors of the same person from different viewpoints is reduced by applying the pose prior. Without the pose prior, the distance between the two descriptors is 1.3216, which has been reduced to 0.8193 after applying the pose prior

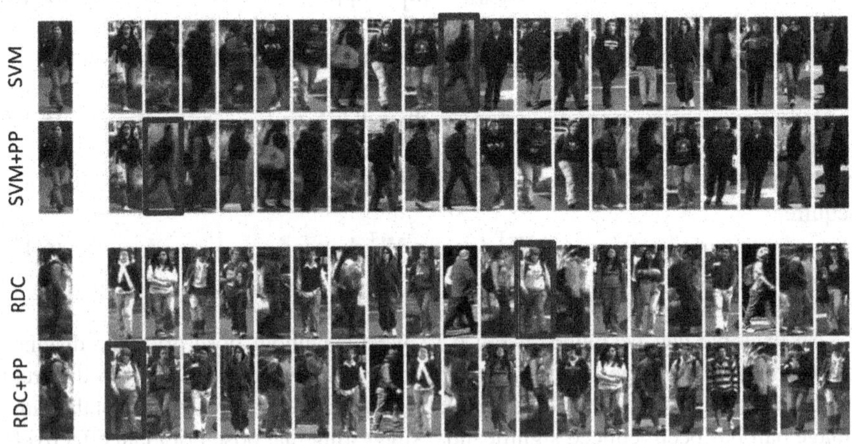

Fig. 6.13 Improvement brought by the pose prior

prior, the true match was promoted to rank 2. Similarly, in the bottom example, the ground truth match was promoted to rank 1 after applying pose prior, from rank 12.

6.4 Experimental Results

We conducted several experiments to evaluate the performance of the proposed algorithm, comparing our algorithm against state-of-the-art competitors on standard benchmarking datasets, as well as a new custom dataset.

6.4.1 Benchmarking Datasets

We tested the performance our algorithm on the ViPER [1], ETHZ [19], i-LIDS [14] and PRID2011 [20] datasets, and compared to other state-of-the-art algorithms including RDC [2], ITM [21] and AdaBoost [1].

The VIPeR dataset contains images of 632 people each taken from two different viewpoints. The ETHZ dataset includes 8555 images of 146 people. The i-LIDS MCTS dataset includes 476 images of 119 people. These three datasets were validated with similar configurations as in [2]. PRID2011 contains 200 person image pairs from two views as well as 734 people appearing in only one of the two views, which was trained and validated with similar configuration as in [20]. Among these datasets, ViPER comes with viewpoint information that can be used to trained the pose prior. We trained pose priors for the other datasets by roughly ground-truthing images into six viewpoint spans. Note that, since images from these datasets have only a small amount of perspective distortion, they were processed without rectification.

We trained and cross-validated the proposed classifier using descriptors extracted with respect to the pose prior under the specific viewpoint. We conducted the experiments with different proportions of training and testing data, and report the results in Tables 6.1 and 6.2. Several of the results for other algorithms are reprinted from [2]. For each probe image, we compute the result of the classifier for all the other images in the gallery set and record the rank of the true match. All results are obtained by averaging ranking results from ten repeated experiments.

We compared our pose prior algorithm (SVM+PP) and its combination with rectification (Combined) to several state-of-art algorithms. From the results, we can see that both the pose prior and person-specific weights can significantly improve the performance of re-identification. Combining the rectification and pose prior methods, the proposed algorithm obtains the best overall results. This is illustrated by a Cumulative Matching Characteristic (CMC) curve for ViPER shown in Fig. 6.14. The experimental results suggest that the proposed algorithm substantially improves the performance of human re-identification on the benchmarking datasets, especially at high ranks.

Table 6.1 Result comparisons on VIPeR and i-LIDS between the proposed algorithms (Combined, SVM+PP) and competitive algorithms

	VIPeR							
Train/Test	316/316				100/512			
Method	1	5	10	20	1	5	10	20
Combined	**22.2**	**46.8**	58.4	**76.0**	**15.03**	**31.6**	**42.1**	**57.3**
SVM+PP	17.9	43.7	**59.5**	74.1	13.5	26.2	39.0	52.9
SVM [18]	16.3	38.2	53.7	69.9	8.9	22.9	32.7	46.0
RDC [2]	15.7	38.4	53.9	69.9	9.1	24.2	34.4	48.6
ITM [21]	11.3	31.4	45.8	63.9	4.2	11.1	17.2	24.6
AdaBoost [1]	8.2	24.2	36.6	52.1	4.2	13.0	20.2	30.7
	i-LIDS							
Train/Test	69/50				39/80			
Method	1	5	10	20	1	5	10	20
Combined	**41.7**	**65.1**	76.9	89.9	33.9	**58.3**	69.1	**82.0**
SVM+PP	37.6	64.2	**77.8**	**91.3**	32.3	56.4	**70.0**	81.9
SVM [18]	37.4	63.0	73.5	88.3	31.7	55.7	67.0	77.8
RDC [2]	37.8	63.7	75.1	88.4	32.6	54.6	65.9	78.3
ITM [21]	29.0	54.0	70.5	86.7	21.7	41.8	55.1	71.3
AdaBoost [1]	29.6	55.2	68.1	82.4	22.8	44.4	57.2	70.6

Each result shows the percentage of the time the correct match occurred in the top k results for a given classifier, where k is the rank

Table 6.2 Result comparisons on ETHZ and PRID2011 between the proposed algorithms (Combined, SVM+PP) and competitive algorithms

	ETHZ							
Train/Test	76/70				26/120			
Method	1	5	10	20	1	5	10	20
Combined	**73.2**	87.2	**94.7**	97.4	64.0	**84.1**	**91.3**	**96.3**
SVM+PP	70.9	86.9	94.5	**98.1**	62.2	82.3	91.1	96.2
SVM [18]	69.1	86.2	92.3	97.1	61.3	78.9	85.9	92.7
RDC [2]	69.0	85.8	92.2	96.9	61.6	79.7	86.7	93.3
ITM [21]	56.3	80.7	88.6	94.1	43.1	66.0	76.6	86.8
AdaBoost [1]	65.6	84.0	90.5	95.6	60.7	78.8	85.7	92.0

PRID2011					
Train/Test	100/100				
Method	1	10	20	50	100
Combined	15.9	**44.7**	52.5	**73.1**	79.2
SVM+PP	13.3	38.4	50.2	72.9	79.3
SVM [18]	13.1	37.2	48.8	64.1	75.8
RDC [2]	12.3	37.8	49.2	63.7	75.2
ITM [21]	15	42	**54**	70	**80**
AdaBoost [1]	4	24	37	56	70

Each result shows the percentage of the time the correct match occurred in the top k results for a given classifier, where k is the rank

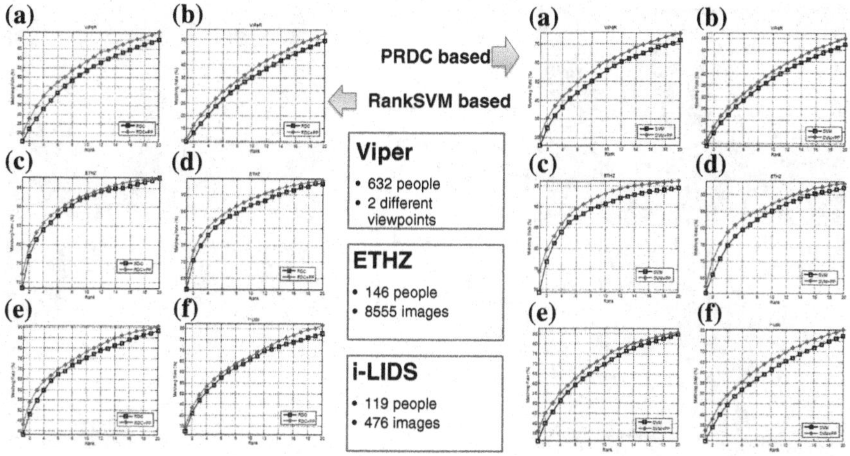

Fig. 6.14 CMC curves for benchmark datasets

6.4.2 Airport Surveillance Camera Experiment

We also tested the algorithms on videos from a surveillance camera network at a medium-sized US airport. We analyzed four synchronized video streams from this camera network, with relative positions sketched in Fig. 6.15.

We indicate a target in one view, and then automatically extract descriptors of the target and detect its reappearance in the other cameras. A collection of rectified target images from the experiment is shown in Fig. 6.15, demonstrating the substantial appearance variation of the target.

We roughly calibrated all the cameras using the embedded function from a Bosch VIP1X encoder by manually labeling parallel lines on the floor. In this way we can rectify the sub-images and obtain the pose angle of all the humans in the videos. While in the benchmarking datasets, the views of each person were generally frontal, the targets in these videos often only appear from the back, so the general matching method with both "Frontal View" $\mathbf{X}_F$ and "Back View" $\mathbf{X}_B$ is used here.

We tagged 86 targets in one of the four cameras. After the target leaves the camera in which he/she was tagged, 50 candidates are selected from the other views, only one of which is a correct match. We compared our proposed algorithm (including SVM with sub-image rectification denoted by SVM+R) to the RDC algorithm [2], the next best performer on the benchmarking datasets above as well as the original SVM algorithm [18]. The results of this more realistic experiment are summarized in Table 6.3. It can be seen that the proposed algorithms outperform RDC and SVM at every rank. It is clear that with the help of the sub-image rectification, the proposed algorithm obtained more obvious advantage over the other algorithms. We conclude that our pose-invariant approach has substantial promise for dealing with the kinds of re-identification problems likely to occur in real-world scenarios.

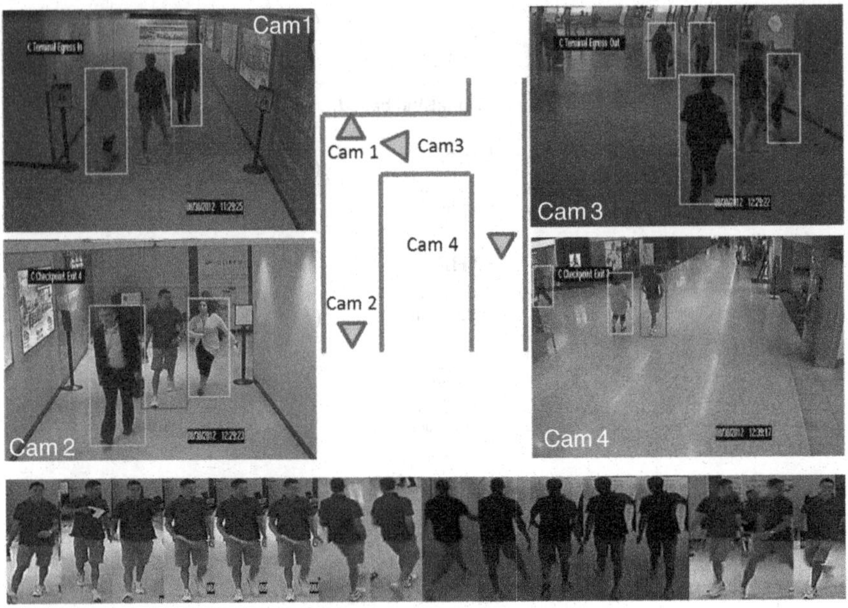

Fig. 6.15 Floor plan and sample images of the camera network used for human re-identification

Table 6.3 Re-identification results comparing the proposed algorithm, SVM and RDC on the difficult airport camera network experiment

Method	1	5	10	20
Combined	**29.7**	**68.4**	**84.3**	**95.1**
SVM+PP	21.2	56.7	76.8	88.7
SVM+R	23.1	64.7	78.0	89.9
SVM [18]	17.2	50.8	66.0	83.6
RDC [2]	17.5	49.4	64.8	83.1

6.5 Discussion

We proposed a new pose prior for making the descriptors of targets more discriminative, in order to improve the performance of human re-identification across cameras. Experimental results on challenging datasets suggest that the proposed algorithm can significantly improve performance and robustness in real-world re-identification problems with lighting and viewpoint changes.

We compared the proposed algorithm to state-of-the-art algorithms; the experimental results suggest that the proposed algorithm can significantly improve the performance of re-identification with current metric learning algorithms. The performance of the proposed algorithms may be degraded when the appearances of all the candidates are similar, or if they move in unusual patterns. To address these issues, one should also consider adding dynamic characteristics to descriptors and continuously learning discriminative features. Calibration-free pose/viewpoint estimation would also be needed to make the algorithm more general.

References

1. D. Gray, Viewpoint invariant pedestrian recognition with an ensemble of localized features, in *European Conference on Computer Vision*, Marseille, France (2008)
2. W. Zheng, S. Gong, T. Xiang, Re-identification by relative distance comparison. IEEE Trans. Pattern Anal. Mach. Intell. **35**, 653–668 (2012)
3. A. Alahi, P. Vandergheynst, M. Bierlaire, M. Kunt, Cascade of descriptors to detect and track objects across any network of cameras. Comput. Vis. Image Underst. **114**, 624–640 (2010)
4. D. Conte, P. Foggia, G. Percannella, M. Vento, A multiview appearance model for people re-identification, in *AVSS*, Klagenfurt, Austria (IEEE, 2011)
5. K.E.A. Van de Sande, T. Gevers, C.G.M. Snoek, Evaluating color descriptors for object and scene recognition. IEEE Trans. Pattern Anal. Mach. Intell. **32**, 1582–1596 (2010)
6. W.R. Schwartz, L.S. Davis, Learning discriminative appearance-based models using partial least squares, in *Brazilian Symposium on Computer Graphics and Image Processing*, Rio de Janeiro, Brazil (IEEE, 2009)
7. W.-S. Zheng, S. Gong, T. Xiang, Associating groups of people, in *British Machine Vision Conference*, London, UK, pp. 23.1–23.11 (2009)
8. B. Ma, Y. Su, F. Jurie, Local descriptors encoded by Fisher vectors for person re-identification, in *ECCV Workshops*, Firenze, Italy, pp. 413–422 (2012)
9. B. Ma, Y. Su, F. Jurie, BiCov: a novel image representation for person re-identification and face verification, in *British Machive Vision Conference*, Guildford, UK (2012)
10. Y. Li, B. Wu, R. Nevatia, Human detection by searching in 3d space using camera and scene knowledge, in *ICPR*, Tampa, Florida (IEEE, 2008)
11. M. Li, Kinematic calibration of an active head-eye system. IEEE Trans. Robot. Autom. **14**(1), 153–158 (1998)
12. A. Torii, M. Havlena, T. Pajdla, B. Leibe, Measuring camera translation by the dominant apical angle, in *IEEE Conference on Computer Vision and Pattern Recognition*, Anchorage, June 2008
13. F. Lv, T. Zhao, R. Nevatia, Camera calibration from video of a walking human. IEEE Trans. Pattern Anal. Mach. Intell. **28**, 1513–1518 (2006)
14. UK Home Office. (26 March 2013). Imagery Library for Intelligent Detection Systems. https://www.gov.uk/government/collections/i-lids. Accessed 2 June 2013
15. Z. Wu, Y. Li, R.J. Radke, Viewpoint invariant human re-identification in real-world camera network using pose priors. IEEE Trans. Pattern Anal. Mach. Intell. **37**, 1095–1108 (2015)
16. T. Joach, Training linear SVMs in linear time, in *ACM SIGKDD International Conference on Knowledge Discovery and Data Mining*, Philadelphia, USA (2006)
17. K.Q. Weinberger, L.K. Saul, Distance metric learning for large margin nearest neighbor classification. J. Mach. Learn. Res. **10**, 207–244 (2009)
18. B. Prosser, W.-S. Zheng, S. Gong, T. Xiang, Person re-identification by support vector ranking, in *BMVC* (2010)
19. A. Ess, B. Leibe, L. Van Gool, Depth and appearance for mobile scene analysis, in *ICCV* (2007)
20. M. Hirzer, C. Beleznai, P.M. Roth, H. Bischof, Person re-identification by descriptive and discriminative classification, in *SCIA'11*, May 2011
21. J.V. Davis, B. Kulis, P. Jain, S. Sra, I.S. Dhillon, Information-theoretic metric learning, in *Proceedings of ICML07* (2007)

Chapter 7
Learning Subject-Discriminative Features

7.1 Online Learning and Matching

In this section, we introduce algorithms for online descriptor extraction and adaptive candidate matching. The online algorithm leverages the pose prior $\mathbf{P}(\theta)$ and classifier $\mathbf{W}$ learned offline using training data in the previous section.

In previous chapters, we discuss offline-learned distance metric $\mathbf{W}$, signatures, and $\mathbf{P}(\theta)$. In this chapter, we are going to dig into boosting human re-identification performance online [1].

7.2 Extracting Signatures

In order to extract viewpoint invariant signatures, we assume the cameras are properly calibrated to the floor plane, and pose prior $\mathbf{P}(\theta)$ is learned. Multiple object tracker is generating proposals (i.e., candidate images, or "probe") while maintaining the tracklets in the camera field of view [2]. With each probe image, the viewpoint angle θ is calculated before the sub-image is rectified. Then the signature can be extracted $\mathbf{X}$. Ideally we want to identify the signature of the person from the frontal view (0°), i.e., $\mathbf{X}_F$. However in real-world scenarios, the frontal view may not be seen initially, or even during the whole time when the person is under tracking. However, given a $\mathbf{X}_{theta_j}$ captured from viewpoint θ_j, $\mathbf{X}_F$ can be roughly estimated via weighting features histograms with pose prior which is ensuring signatures extracted from any viewpoint to be similar.

The classifier model we trained offline is a general model, which is universal for every human [3–6]. However, learning discriminative features for the particular target being tracked may greatly boost the performance of the re-identification [1, 7]. That is, we update the classifier function to

$$f(\mathbf{d}) = \mathbf{W}^\top \mathbf{d} + \alpha \mathbf{s}^\top \mathbf{d} \qquad (7.1)$$

Z. Wu, *Human Re-Identification*, Multimedia Systems and Applications,
DOI 10.1007/978-3-319-40991-7_7

where α is a weighting factor and $\mathbf{s}$ is a person-specific weight on the descriptor. We first model the distribution of each feature with a Gaussian, based on offline training data; denote the mean and variance of feature i in the descriptor $\mathbf{X}$ as $\hat{\mu}(i)$ and $\hat{\sigma}(i)$:

$$\hat{\mu}(i) = \frac{\sum_{j=1}^{N}(1+\cos\frac{\theta_j}{2})\mathbf{X}_j}{(\sum_{j=1}^{N}\cos\frac{\theta_j}{2})+N} \tag{7.2}$$

$$\hat{\sigma}^2(i) = \frac{\sum_{j=1}^{N}(1+\cos\frac{\theta_j}{2})(\mathbf{X}_j-\hat{\mu}(i))^2}{(\sum_{j=1}^{N}\cos\frac{\theta_j}{2})+N} \tag{7.3}$$

in which $\mathbf{X}_j$ and θ_j are the descriptor and viewpoint respectively of the jth training sample, and $\cos\frac{\theta_j}{2}$ is a weighting term for images captured from different viewpoint angles θ_j. During online processing, once the target is tagged and descriptors $\mathbf{X}_F$ are extracted, we find the features i that have low likelihood with respect to the offline Gaussian distribution. That is, we find the person-specific features that we would not expect based on the training data; these are particularly discriminative for that person. We explicitly determine $\mathbf{s}$ by first computing

$$\tilde{\mathbf{s}}(i) = \begin{cases} 1 - G(\mathbf{X}_F(i), \hat{\mu}(i), \hat{\sigma}(i)) & G(\cdot) < \tau \\ 0 & \text{otherwise} \end{cases} \tag{7.4}$$

in which the Gaussian function $G(\cdot)$ is normalized to have height 1. In our experiments, we used $\tau = 0.1$. This is because we consider the features with lower probability in the distribution of training data as more discriminative, or unique. After processing all the features in $\mathbf{X}_F$, we compute

$$\mathbf{s} = \mathbf{W} \circ \frac{\tilde{\mathbf{s}}}{\|\tilde{\mathbf{s}}\|}$$

where $\circ$ is the element product. Finally, we learn α from the training data using

$$\alpha = \frac{1}{N}\sum_{j=1}^{N}\delta(\mathbf{s}_j^\top \mathbf{d}_{\text{same}} < \mathbf{s}_j^\top \mathbf{d}_{\text{diff}}) \tag{7.5}$$

where $\delta(S) = 1$ if statement S is true and 0 otherwise. Figure 7.1 illustrates the process of offline training and online learning of discriminative features. Note that the discriminative features can be learned with a single image. The overall process of learning the classifier for the target is shown in Fig. 7.2.

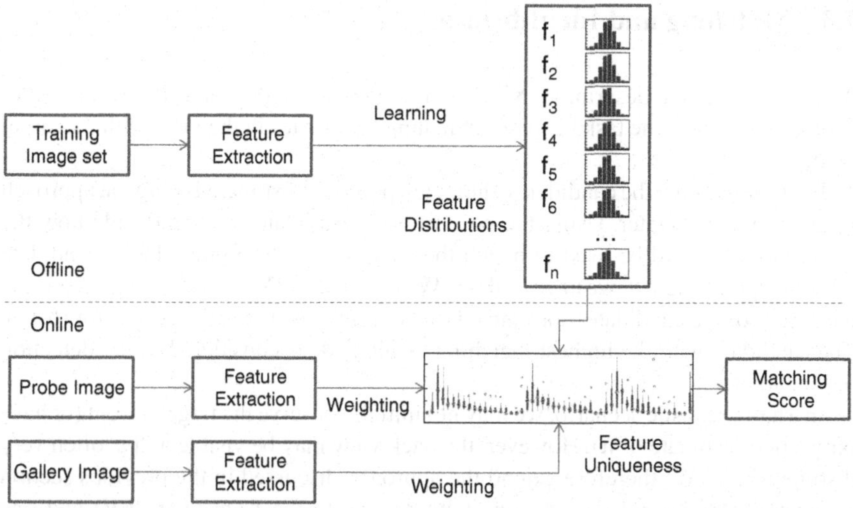

Fig. 7.1 Illustration of learning discriminative features

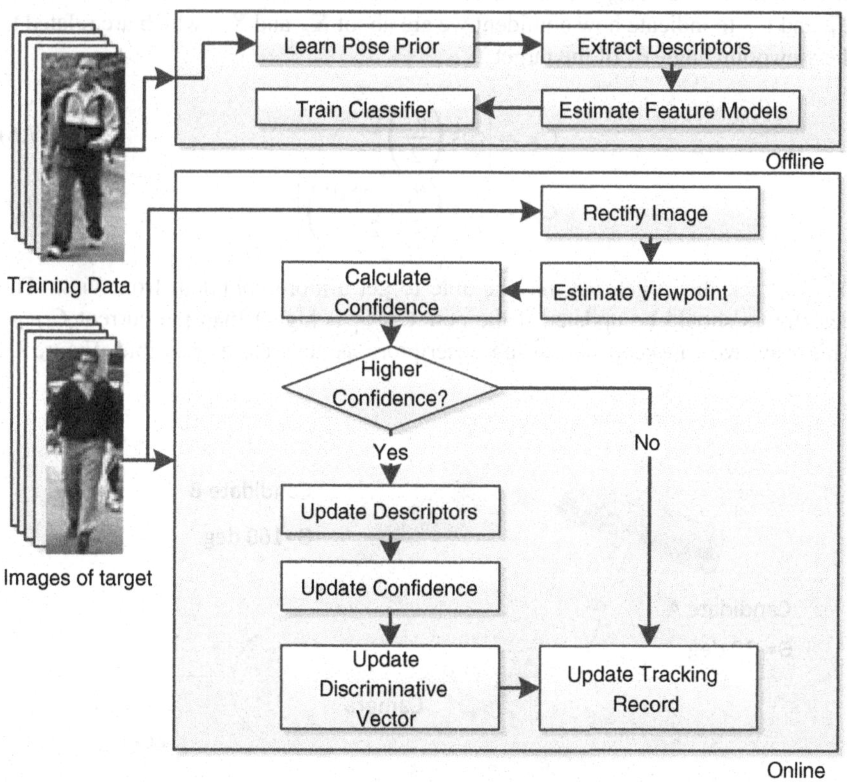

Fig. 7.2 Flowchart of offline and online learning processes

7.3 Matching and Identification

After extracting the descriptors $\mathbf{X}_F^t$ the target may leave the current view and enter another view. Now the task becomes matching candidates in the view with the target model.

First, by tracking the candidates, their viewpoints are estimated using the approach in the previous chapter. Using the pose of each candidate, we can decide how the target model should be used to match the candidates' descriptors. For a candidate with viewpoint angle θ, we have $f(\mathbf{d}) = \mathbf{W}^\top \mathbf{d}$ with $\mathbf{d} = |\mathbf{X}_F^t - \mathbf{X}_F^c|$, where $\mathbf{X}_F^c$ is the descriptor of the candidate, normalized to the front view using the pose prior (6.15). The candidate with the highest matching result $f(\mathbf{d})$ is considered as the detection of the target.

In a more realistic scenario, we may not initially observe the target's front (or have only a poor estimate of it). However, the back view may be visible and is often very distinguishing. We therefore extend the approach discussed in the previous section by computing two pose priors: one with respect to the front view (FV) and one with respect to the back view (BV). We similarly estimate the descriptor $\mathbf{X}_B$ and discriminative vector $\mathbf{s}_B$ for the back view. Additionally, we introduce parameters C_F and C_B to indicate how confident we are about $\mathbf{X}_F$ and $\mathbf{X}_B$, which are related to the viewpoint angle θ_j of the target

$$C_F = \left|\cos\left(\frac{\theta_j}{2}\right)\right| \tag{7.6}$$

$$C_B = \left|\cos\left(\frac{\theta_j - 180^\circ}{2}\right)\right| \tag{7.7}$$

As we track the target, we may be able to get a more confident front view. The descriptors should be updated if the new $C_{\{F,B\}}$ is higher than the current $C_{\{F,B\}}$. This way, we can keep our stored descriptors as accurate as possible. Figure 7.3

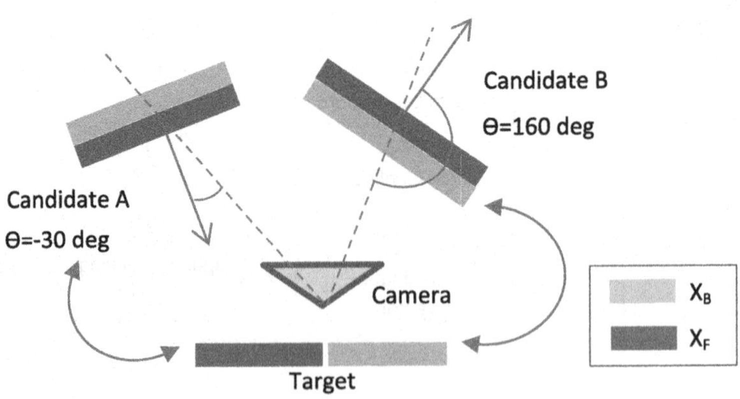

Fig. 7.3 Illustration of online matching

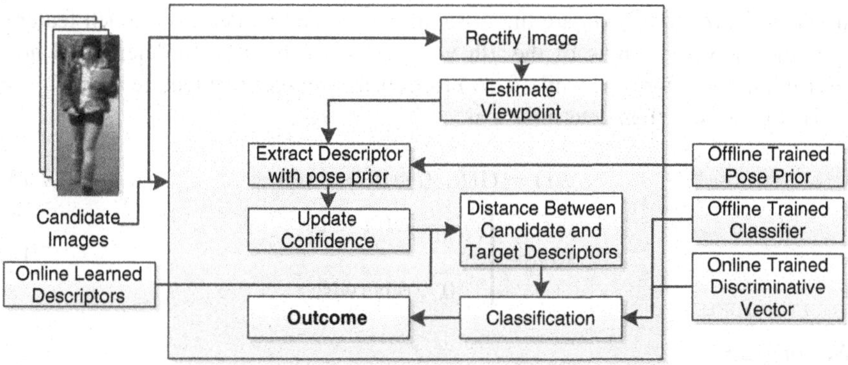

Fig. 7.4 Flowchart of general online re-identification processes

illustrates matching under the more general scenario. A candidate with a viewpoint angle of θ can be matched with the target model by

$$f(\mathbf{d}) = f_F(\mathbf{d})\cos^2\frac{\theta}{2} + f_B(\mathbf{d})\sin^2\frac{\theta}{2} \tag{7.8}$$

in which

$$f_{\{F,B\}}(\mathbf{d}) = (\mathbf{W} + \alpha\mathbf{s}_{\{F,B\}})^\top\mathbf{d} \tag{7.9}$$

$$\mathbf{d} = |\mathbf{X}^t_{\{F,B\}} - \mathbf{X}^c_{\{F,B\}}| \tag{7.10}$$

The process for online matching is shown in Fig. 7.4.

7.4 Multi-shot Online Learning and Matching

Since we usually can obtain multiple images of the target under tracking, we can learn the Subject-Discriminative Features in a more robust way. First we estimate the in-class statistics with descriptors $\mathbf{X}_j$ extracted from $j = 1\ldots n$ views of the target

$$\hat{\mu}_{in}(i) = \frac{\sum_{j=1}^{n}(1+\cos\frac{\theta_j}{2})\mathbf{X}_j(u)}{\sum_{j=1}^{n}\cos\frac{\theta_j}{2} + n} \tag{7.11}$$

$$\hat{\sigma}^2_{in}(i) = \frac{\sum_{j=1}^{n}(1+\cos\frac{\theta_j}{2})(\mathbf{X}_j - \hat{\mu_{in}}(i))^2}{\sum_{j=1}^{n}\cos\frac{\theta_j}{2} + n - 1} \tag{7.12}$$

in which $\hat{\mu}_{in}(i)$ and $\hat{\sigma}^2_{in}(i)$ are the in-sample mean and variance of the ith feature. θ_j is the viewpoint angle of the jth view. $\hat{\mu}(i)$ can be used to determined how discriminative feature i is while $\hat{\mu}_{in}(i)$ reflects how descriptive feature i is.

That is, we can then determine **s** as

$$v(i) = G(\hat{\mu}_{in}(i), \hat{\mu}(i), \hat{\sigma}(i)) \tag{7.13}$$

$$\tilde{\mathbf{s}}(i) = \begin{cases} \frac{1-v(i)}{\hat{\sigma}_{in}(i)} & v(i) < \tau \\ 0 & \text{otherwise} \end{cases} \tag{7.14}$$

We compute

$$\mathbf{s} = \mathbf{W} \circ \frac{\tilde{\mathbf{s}}}{||\tilde{\mathbf{s}}||}$$

Then we can learn α from the training data by

$$\alpha = \frac{1}{N_m} \sum_i \sum_j \delta(\mathbf{s}^\top \mathbf{d}^i_{\text{same}} < \mathbf{s}^\top \mathbf{d}^j_{\text{diff}}) \tag{7.15}$$

In which $\mathbf{d}_{\text{same}}$ is the distance of two descriptors of the target. $N_m = \sum_i \sum_j \cdot$ $\mathbf{d}_{\text{diff}}$ is the distance between one target descriptor and one nontarget descriptor from the training samples. In our experiments, we used $\tau = 0.3$. For each target k, we also estimate $\mathbf{s}_k$ and α_k. $\mathbf{X}_k$, $\mathbf{s}_k$ and α_k are updated every time a new view of the target k is observed.

7.5 Discussion

Metric learning algorithms during the offline learning process are actually minimizing the in-sample error and maximizing the inter-sample error of the training set. In other words, they are learning the importance of each feature. Features with high weight are the most discriminative and descriptive features based on the training set. The weights are considered generally applicable to all targets; however, this is not necessarily for everyone. In this chapter, we show that for each target of interest online, we can also learn his/her person-specific discriminative features.

References

1. Z. Wu, Y. Li, R.J. Radke, Viewpoint invariant human re-identification in real-world camera network using pose priors. IEEE Trans. Pattern Anal. Mach. Intell. **37**, 1095–1108 (2015)
2. F. Lv, T. Zhao, R. Nevatia, Camera calibration from video of a walking human. IEEE Trans. Pattern Anal. Mach. Intell. **28**, 1513–1518 (2006)

3. W. Zheng, S. Gong, T. Xiang, Re-identification by relative distance comparison. IEEE Trans. Pattern Anal. Mach. Intell. **35**, 653–668 (2012)
4. B. Prosser, W.-S. Zheng, S. Gong, T. Xiang, Person Re-Identification by Support Vector Ranking, in *BMVC* (2010)
5. K.E.A. Van de Sande, T. Gevers, C.G.M. Snoek, Evaluating color descriptors for object and scene recognition. IEEE Trans. Pattern Anal. Mach. Intell. **32**, 1582–1596 (2010)
6. B. Ma, Y. Su, F. Jurie, Local descriptors encoded by fisher vectors for person re-identification, in *ECCV Workshops* (Firenze, Italy 2012), pp. 413–422
7. M. Hirzer, C. Beleznai, P.M. Roth, H. Bischof, Person re-identification by descriptive and discriminative classification, in *SCIA'11* (2011)

Chapter 8
Dimension Reduction with Random Projections

Signatures used in human reidentification problems are usually of high dimension, ranging from 2,000 to 10,000. While a higher dimensional feature vector usually results in better performance since it is capturing more information, the training process is going to take a very long time, making online training and refinement less feasible. In this chapter, we are going to talk about an approach to significantly reduce the dimensionality of the signatures with the help of random projection and random forest.

8.1 Random Projection

Random projection [1–5] is an approach for dimensionality reduction for given dataset in Euclidean space while preserving distances. Let $\mathbf{X}$ be the feature vector set of a training dataset consisting N samples:

$$\mathbf{X} = \{x_1, x_2, \ldots, x_i, \ldots, x_N\} \tag{8.1}$$

where x_i is the feature vector for the ith sample with the dimensionality of n. Let the target dimensionality be m with $m << n$, we can use a random matrix $\mathbf{P}_{m\times n}$ to project the original feature vectors into a m dimensional subspace:

$$\mathbf{X}' = \mathbf{P}_{m\times n}\mathbf{X} \tag{8.2}$$

where $\mathbf{X}'$ is the $m \times N$ dimension subspace projection of $\mathbf{X}$. The Euclidean distance of two signatures $\mathbf{x}_1$ and $\mathbf{x}_2$ becomes:

$$\begin{aligned} d(\mathbf{x}_1, \mathbf{x}_2) &= \|\mathbf{x}_1 - \mathbf{x}_2\| &(8.3)\\ &= s\|\mathbf{P}\mathbf{x}_1 - \mathbf{P}\mathbf{x}_2\| &(8.4)\end{aligned}$$

Z. Wu, *Human Re-Identification*, Multimedia Systems and Applications,
DOI 10.1007/978-3-319-40991-7_8

where s is a scale factor

$$s = \left(\frac{n}{m}\right)^{\frac{1}{2}} \tag{8.5}$$

Let p_{ij} be the element at (i, j) in $\mathbf{P}_{m\times n}$, the selection of p_{ij} can be randomly drawn from normal distribution with $\mu = 0$ and $\sigma = 1$. Alternatively, it can be simplified as:

$$p_{ij} = \begin{cases} 1 & \text{with probablity } \frac{1}{6} \\ 0 & \text{with probablity } \frac{4}{6} \\ -1 & \text{with probablity } \frac{1}{6} \end{cases} \tag{8.6}$$

Usually $\mathbf{P}_{m\times n}$ needs to be orthogonalized [6]. Although it has been shown that vectors p_i in projection matrix P are not necessarily orthogonal [1] in general, the random projector in theorem [6] is orthogonal. In this chapter, the vectors in random projection matrices are orthonormal. The signatures after random projection denoted by

$$\mathbf{X}' = \{x'_1, x'_2, \ldots, x'_N\}. \tag{8.7}$$

8.2 Random Forest

Random forest [7–10], also called randomized decision forests, is a machine learning method that is trained with randomized selection of features from training samples on an ensemble of un-pruned decision trees learners:

$$\mathbf{T} = \{\mathbf{t}_1, \mathbf{t}_2, \ldots, \mathbf{t}_i, \ldots, \mathbf{t}_n\} \tag{8.8}$$

where $\mathbf{t}_i$ is the ith decision tree. Random forest utilizes a bootstrapping aggregation strategy, that is, it is creating new training sets by randomly sampling the full training set with replacements. Each decision tree learner is independently trained with different bootstrapping samples. The output decision is based on the mean prediction for regression problem, or the class label obtaining most votes for classification problems. Another randomization process of random forest is, it is selecting a random subset of k predictors at each split to reduce variance and improve accuracy, while significantly speeding up the training process.

Random Forest can provide high accuracy in classification, and it can handle large training dataset efficiently. More importantly, it does not overfit, and the forests trained can be used on other datasets.

8.3 Random Forest Pairwise Distance

Human reidentification problem is not exactly formulated as a classification problem. With simple adaptation, Random Forests can also be used as a pairwise metric [11]. Given a Random Forest $\mathbf{T}$, and training samples $\mathbf{S} = \{\mathbf{S}_n \cup \mathbf{S}_f\}$, where

$$\mathbf{S}_n = \{\mathbf{d} = \|\mathbf{X}_i - \mathbf{X}_j\| | i \text{ and } j \text{ are the same person}\} \tag{8.9}$$

and

$$\mathbf{S}_f = \{\mathbf{d} = \|\mathbf{X}_i - \mathbf{X}_j\| | i \text{ and } j \text{ are the different persons}\} \tag{8.10}$$

The target distance assigned to the training samples are:

$$y_i = \begin{cases} 1 \text{ if } \mathbf{s}_i \in \mathbf{S}_f \\ 0 \text{ if } \mathbf{s}_i \in \mathbf{S}_n \end{cases} \tag{8.11}$$

The metric problem can be re-defined as a two-class classification problem, i.e., for each decision tree t_k, the output is in the form of:

$$y_k = t_k \{\mathscr{D}(\|\mathbf{X}_i - \mathbf{X}_j\|)\} \tag{8.12}$$

where $\mathscr{D}$ is the transfer function (mapping function) inputting the sample $\mathbf{s}_i$ into the decision tree, e.g. considering relative location as well as absolute position of the two signatures [11]:

$$\mathscr{D}(\mathbf{X}_i, \mathbf{X}_j) = \begin{bmatrix} |\mathbf{X}_i - \mathbf{X}_j| \\ \frac{\mathbf{X}_i + \mathbf{X}_j}{2} \end{bmatrix} \tag{8.13}$$

By aggregating the decisions from all decision trees, a final "decision" y can be simply given by:

$$y = \frac{1}{n} \sum_{k=1}^{n} t_k \{\mathscr{D}(\mathbf{X}_i, \mathbf{X}_j)\} \tag{8.14}$$

Here the decision is actually the distance for sample $(\mathbf{X}_i, \mathbf{X}_j)$, which fits right into the human reidentification problem. Since a voting scheme is used in calculating the distance, more sophisticated and robust approach in aggregating predictions of the decision trees can be used to effectively remove outliers, such as computing median value, finding the mode of predictions, or fitting a normal distribution.

8.4 Multiple Random-Projection-Based Random Forest Algorithm

Although Random Forest is efficient, the speed in training stage will still suffer from high data dimensionality. As we discussed before, Random Projection can reduce the feature dimension effectively yet preserving distances. However the smaller desire dimension m of feature vector after projection is, more information from the signatures we are losing. In other words, while we are trying to speed up training process, we are compromising on accuracy.

This is a trade-off, but below we are going to introduce an approach to significantly improve training efficiency without losing accuracy, by combining Random Projection and Random Forest metric.

Random Projection is projecting feature vector into subspace with a randomly generated projection base, which should produce no bias. However with different projection bases, the reduced feature vectors contains different portions of information of the original feature vector. By using multiple projections bases, larger portion of the original feature vector $\mathbf{X}$ can be preserved. Each projection base P_i generates a new training set $\mathbf{X}_i'$ with reduced dimension, which can be fed into Random Forest metric to learn a metric $\mathscr{D}_i$. Finally distances output from all Random Forest metrics can be aggregated. We call this approach Random Projection Random Forest (RPRF) [12], which is shown in Algorithm 2.

Algorithm 2: Learning the random forest classifier with multiple random projections

Input: R: number of random projections
$\{x_1, x_2, \ldots, x_N\}$: signatures extracted from each sub-image from training set
$\{l_1, l_2, \ldots, l_N\}, l_i \in \mathbf{C}$: label for each signature
m: projected reduced-dimension number
Output: A set of random forests $\{\mathbf{f}_r\}, r = 1, \ldots, R$

```
for r = 1 to R do
    Generate an n × m orthoprojector matrix P_r;
    Calculate reduced-dimention signatures x'_i = P_r^T x_i, i = 1, ..., N;
    for each signature pair (x'_i, x'_j), i > j do
        if l_i ≠ l_j then
            move (x'_i, x'_j) to set 𝒟;
        else
            move (x'_i, x'_j) to set 𝒮;
        end
    end
    Randomly sample k elements from 𝒮 and 𝒟 without replacement, s.t. |𝒮| = |𝒟|;
    Form 𝒞 = {θ(u, v), y} with (8.11), where (u, v) ∈ 𝒮 ∪ 𝒟;
    Train random forest f_r with constraint set 𝒞;
end
```

Again, a straightforward way to aggregate the output from all Random Forest metrics:

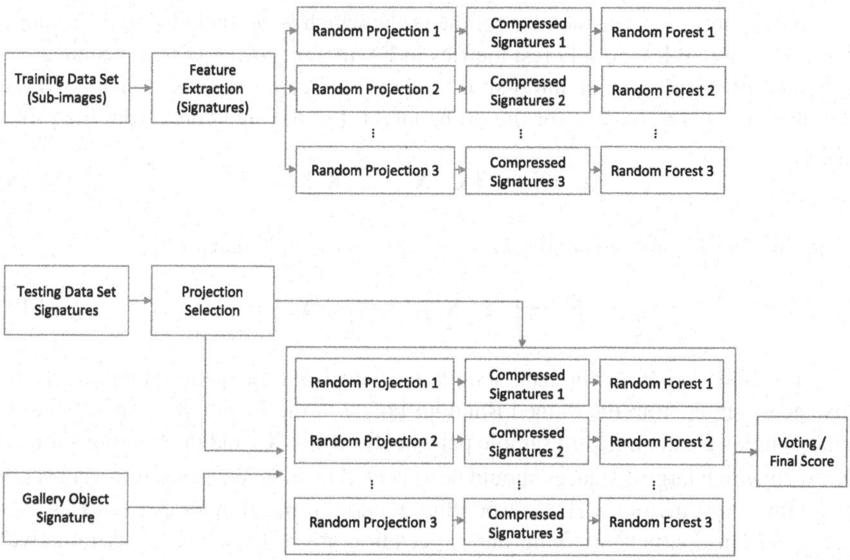

Fig. 8.1 Flowchart of the proposed algorithm

$$\mathbf{F} = \{\mathbf{f}_1, \mathbf{f}_2, \ldots, \mathbf{f}_r\} \tag{8.15}$$

can be defined as Eq. (8.16)

$$y = \frac{1}{h \times n} \sum_{r=1}^{h} \sum_{k=1}^{n} t_{(r,k)} \left(\mathscr{D}(\mathbf{X}_i, \mathbf{X}_j) \right) \tag{8.16}$$

where $t_{(r,k)}$ is the kth decision tree in the rth Random Forest. The overall process of RPRF is shown in Fig. 8.1.

8.5 Target-Specific Discriminative Forests

Like most metric learning algorithms used in human reidentification problems, RFRP is trained offline. When it is online, when a probe image (or sequence) signature $\mathbf{X}_p$ is obtained, we obtain the distance between $\mathbf{X}_p$ and each signature in the gallery set by

$$y_i = \frac{1}{h \times n} \sum_{r=1}^{h} \sum_{k=1}^{n} t_{(r,k)} \left(\mathscr{D}_r(\mathbf{X}_i, \mathbf{X}_p) \right) \tag{8.17}$$

However as we discussed before, each random projection base we used in generating reduced training dataset is capturing different portion of features in the original feature vector. They can be considered representative for the training subjects. However it may not always be the case for the probe which is not included in the training set. Hence not all Random Forest metrics in $\mathbf{F}$ will generate consistent distances.

However in the case of multi-shot scenario, we can learn a subset $\mathbf{F}'$ of $\mathbf{F}$ so that they are discriminative for the probe target. Let the signatures from the probe sequence be:

$$\tilde{\mathbf{X}}_p = \{\mathbf{X}_1, \mathbf{X}_2, \ldots, \mathbf{X}_c\} \tag{8.18}$$

from this set of probe signatures, we can construct sample pairs as

$$\tilde{\mathbf{S}}_c = \left\{(\mathbf{X}_i, \mathbf{X}_j)|\mathbf{X}_i, \mathbf{X}_j \in \tilde{\mathbf{X}}_p\right\} \tag{8.19}$$

Since both signatures in each sample pair are from the same probe target, the distances output from the trained Random Forest in the $\mathbf{F}$ should be small. On the other hand, we can also form sample pairs set $\tilde{\mathbf{S}}_f$ using $\tilde{\mathbf{X}}_p$ and the training subjects $\tilde{\mathbf{X}}_t$, with which large distances should be expected from $\mathbf{F}$. We can select a subset of Random Forest metrics and corresponding random projection bases from $\mathbf{F}$, which are generating output satisfying our expectation above to be the "discriminative" subset of RFRP, denoted by $\mathbf{F}_d$, for probe subject. This can be done by setting a threshold on the statistics of distances output from each $\mathbf{f}_i \in \mathbf{F}$:

$$\tau_i = \frac{p(\mathbf{f}_i(\mathbf{s}) = 1|\mathbf{s} \in \tilde{\mathbf{S}}_f)}{p(\mathbf{f}_i(\mathbf{s}) = 0|\mathbf{s} \in \tilde{\mathbf{S}}_c)} \tag{8.20}$$

The process of learning online discriminative RFRP is shown in Algorithm 3.

Algorithm 3: Personally Discriminative Random Forest Selection

---

Input: $\{P_1, P_2, \ldots, P_R\}$: random projection matrices
$\{\mathbf{T}_1, \mathbf{T}_2, \ldots, \mathbf{T}_R\}$: trained random forests
$\{\tilde{x}_1, \tilde{x}_2, \ldots, \tilde{x}_M\}, \tilde{x}_i \in \mathbb{R}^n$: feature vectors extracted from multi-shot images of a person
$\{x_1, x_2, \ldots, x_N\}, x_i \in \mathbb{R}^n$: feature vectors in the training set
Output: random forest set $\{\mathbf{T}_{r'}\} \subset \{\mathbf{T}_1, \mathbf{T}_2, \ldots, \mathbf{T}_R\}$
for $r = 1$ *to* R **do**
  Compute dimensionally reduced feature vectors $\tilde{x}'_i = P_r^\top \tilde{x}_i, i = 1, \ldots, M$, and $x'_i = P_r^\top x_i, i = 1, \ldots, N$;
  for *each data pair* $(\tilde{x}'_i, \tilde{x}'_j), i > j$ **do**
    Calculate similarity score $\tilde{y}_{ij}$;
  end
  Average all $\tilde{y}_{ij}$ to get positive-pair similarity score Y_r^+;
  for *each data pair* $(\tilde{x}'_i, x'_j), i = 1, \ldots, M, j = 1, \ldots, N$ **do**
    Calculate similarity score y_{ij} ;
  end
  Average all y_{ij} to get negative-pair similarity score Y_r^-;
  Score ratio $\sigma_r = \frac{Y_r^+}{Y_r^-}$
end
Find the random projection trees $\mathbf{T}_{r'}$, whose score ratio $\sigma_{r'} > mean\{\sigma_r\}, r = 1, \ldots, R$;
Return $\{\mathbf{T}_{r'}\}$;

Define the set $\mathscr{R} = \{r'\}$, where r' collects the indices of the selected random forests from Algorithm 3. Then, Eq. (8.16) can be updated as

$$Y = \frac{1}{|\mathscr{R}|K} \sum_{r' \in \mathscr{R}} \sum_{k=1}^{K} t_k^{r'} (\theta(u, v)) \tag{8.21}$$

where $u \in \tilde{\mathbf{X}}$ which is used to select the appropriate person-discriminative random forests $\{\mathbf{T}_{r'}\}$. Figure 8.1 illustrates the overall method.

8.6 Discussion

In this chapter, we introduce a novel approach combining the process of reducing the dimensionality of the signatures, and learning the discriminative metric. The proposed RPRF approach has the advantages of both random projection and random forest, which can significantly reduce the training time, while not scarifying performance. The online selection of person-specific classifiers subset further improves the robustness and adaptability of the system.

References

1. E. Bingham, H. Mannila, Random projection in dimensionality reduction: applications to image and text data, in *ACMSIGKDD* (2001)
2. T. Takiguchi, J. Bilmes, M. Yoshii, Y. Ariki, Evaluation of random-projection-based feature combination on speech recognition, in *2010 IEEE International Conference on Acoustics, Speech and Signal Processing*, 2010, pp. 2150–2153
3. A. Ahmad, G. Brown, Random projection random discretization ensembles -ensembles of linear multivariate decision trees. IEEE Trans. Knowl. Data Eng. **26**(5), 1225–1239 (2014)
4. V. Sulic, J. Pers, M. Kristan, S. Kovacic, Dimensionality reduction for distributed vision systems using random projection, in *2010 20th International Conference on Pattern Recognition*, 2010, pp. 380–383
5. B. Xu, G. Qiu, Crowd density estimation based on rich features and random projection forest, in *IEEE Winter Conference on Applications of Computer Vision*, 2016, pp. 1–8
6. R. Baraniuk, M. Wakin, Random projections of smooth manifolds. Found. Comput. Math. **9**(1), 51–77 (2009)
7. G. Rogez, J. Rihan, S. Ramalingam, C. Orrite, P.H.S. Torr, Randomized trees for human pose detection, in *IEEE Conference on Computer Vision and Pattern Recognition*, 2008, pp. 1–8
8. A.G. Schwing, C. Zach, Y. Zheng, M. Pollefeys, Adaptive random forest–How many "experts" to ask before making a decision? in *IEEE Conference on Computer Vision and Pattern Recognition*, 2011, pp. 1377–1384
9. X. Liu et al., Semi-supervised node splitting for random forest construction, in *IEEE Conference on Computer Vision and Pattern Recognition*, 2013, pp. 492–499
10. G. Yu, J. Yuan, Z. Liu, Unsupervised random forest indexing for fast action search, in *IEEE Conference on Computer Vision and Pattern Recognition*, 2011, pp. 865–872

11. C. Xiong, D. Johnson, R. Xu, J.J. Corso, Random forests for metric learning with implicit pairwise position dependence, in *ACMSIGKDD* (2012)
12. Y. Li, Z. Wu, R.J. Radke, Multi-shot re-identification with random-projection-based random forest, in *IEEE Winter Conference on Applications of Computer Vision*, 2015

Chapter 9
Sample Selection for Multi-shot Human Re-identification

In real-world human re-identification applications, "probes" are usually more than one image of a candidate, also known as multi-shot re-identification problem, since in most of the cases, a candidate is being tracked by a multi-object tracker through out his/her presence in the view of a camera.

9.1 Discriminant Dimensionality Reduction

The feature vectors employed in the re-id problem are usually high dimensional, leading to sparse sample points in the feature space. Thus it is necessary to find the intrinsic low-dimensional space, such that samples from the same person stay close to each other while far apart from those belonging to different persons. This coincide with the Fisher criterion [1],

$$J = \mathrm{Tr}\left((\boldsymbol{T}^\top \boldsymbol{S}^w \boldsymbol{T})^{-1} \boldsymbol{T}^\top \boldsymbol{S}^b \boldsymbol{T}\right) \tag{9.1}$$

where $\boldsymbol{T}$ is the linear transformation matrix that projects data samples onto a low-dimensional subspace. $\boldsymbol{S}^w$ and $\boldsymbol{S}^b$ are the within-class scatter matrix and between-class scatter matrix respectively.

Maximizing above equation to find a matrix $\boldsymbol{T}$ is known as Fisher Discriminant Analysis (FDA) [1], and it works well for unimodal data. However, in the re-id problem, the goal is to match person based on images captured from different cameras. Because of viewpoint and environmental variation, the appearance of the same person from these two cameras should be inherently different. Thus the data samples in the feature space can easily split into two clusters, which means the data from each person is "multi-modal". We randomly select three persons to plot their data points in the first two principal dimensions. It is clear that data extracted from different cameras are well separated. In such case, if FDA technique is applied it will try to merge

Z. Wu, *Human Re-Identification*, Multimedia Systems and Applications,
DOI 10.1007/978-3-319-40991-7_9

clusters for each person. This is a harder requirement than simply keeping samples within each cluster close, and may leave less dimensionality for separating different classes. We applied Local Fisher Discriminant Analysis (LFDA) [2] to mitigate this issue.

LFDA combines the idea of Fisher Discriminant Analysis (FDA) [1] and Locality Preserving Projections (LPP) [3] to satisfy the Fisher criterion while preserving local structures. It is shown that the within-class scatter matrix and the between-class scatter matrix in Eq. 9.1 can be expressed as

$$\boldsymbol{S}^{w} = \frac{1}{2}\sum_{i,j=1}^{N} \boldsymbol{W}^{w}_{i,j}(x_i - x_j)(x_i - x_j)^{\top}, \tag{9.2}$$

$$\boldsymbol{S}^{b} = \frac{1}{2}\sum_{i,j=1}^{N} \boldsymbol{W}^{b}_{i,j}(x_i - x_j)(x_i - x_j)^{\top}, \tag{9.3}$$

where

$$\boldsymbol{W}^{w}_{i,j} = \begin{cases} \boldsymbol{A}_{i,j}/n_c & \textit{if } y_i = y_j = c, \\ 0 & \textit{if } y_i \neq y_j, \end{cases} \tag{9.4}$$

$$\boldsymbol{W}^{b}_{i,j} = \begin{cases} \boldsymbol{A}_{i,j}(1/N - 1/n_c) & \textit{if } y_i = y_j = c, \\ 1/N & \textit{if } y_i \neq y_j. \end{cases} \tag{9.5}$$

For FDA, the weighting $\boldsymbol{A}_{i,j} = 1$, which indicates if two sample points $\{x_i, x_j\}$ are from the same class c, their contribution to the scatter matrices takes a constant weight. However, when the data is multi-modal within the class, all the data is actually forced into one cluster, and this is too restrictive. To keep the local structure of data, LFDA superimposes the affinity matrix $\boldsymbol{A}$ defined in [3] to weightings $\boldsymbol{W}^{w}$ and $\boldsymbol{W}^{b}$, where $\boldsymbol{A}_{ij} \in [0, 1]$ is the affinity between x_i and x_j. A larger value indicates a higher similarity.

The LFDA transformation matrix $\boldsymbol{T}$ can be obtained by maximizing Eq. 9.1. The solution can be determined from the generalized eigenvalue problem,

$$\boldsymbol{S}^{b}\varphi = \lambda \boldsymbol{S}^{w}\varphi, \tag{9.6}$$

where $\{\varphi_i\}_{i=1}^{d}$ are the eigenvectors and $\lambda_1 \geq \lambda_2 \geq \cdots \geq \lambda_d$ are the associated eigenvalues. Then $\boldsymbol{T}$ is given by

$$\boldsymbol{T} = [\varphi_1|\varphi_2|\ldots|\varphi_m]. \tag{9.7}$$

9.2 Image Sequence Clustering

Now let us take a close look at image sequences. Depending on the video frame rate, it can be temporally dense such that adjacent images exhibit few differences, but across the whole sequence there are several distinctive states. Each state can be represented as a cluster of images. If all the data samples of a person are treated equally, our representation will be highly biased, because there are redundant and noisy information unevenly distributed in different clusters. For instance, a person may stay at one state for a while, there can be clusters consists of occlusions, illumination changes can cause high variance within a cluster, and the number of data samples in each cluster is different.

Thus using all the data samples to find a transformation matrix as discussed in Sect. 9.1 will lead to suboptimal results. Instead, we propose an algorithm that iteratively clusters each image sequence and learn the transformation matrix at the same time [4].

Algorithm 4: Adaptive Local Fisher Discriminative Analysis

Input: $X = (X_1|X_2|\ldots|X_P)$ where X_i contains data samples of person i
$Y = (Y_1|Y_2|\ldots|Y_P)$ where Y_i contains class labels corresponding to data samples of person i
Output: T: transformation matrix
T_{new} = LFDA(X, Y);
Initialize cluster labels C_i of data samples for each person i based on cameras ;
Initialize $J_{new} = 1$, $J = 0$;
while $J_{new} > J$ **do**
  $T = T_{new}$;
  $Z = T^\top * X$;
  foreach *person i* **do**
    C_i = HFGC(Z_i, C_i);
    foreach *cluster label c in unique*(C_i) **do**
      $\bar{x}_i^c = \frac{1}{n_c}\sum_{k=1}^{n_c} x_i^k$, where $c_i^k = c$;
      $\bar{y}_i^c = y_i^k$, $y_i^k \in Y_i$ are same;
    end
  end
  T_{new} = LFDA($\bar{X}, \bar{Y}$);
  Calculate J in Eq. 9.1 using T;
  Calculate J_{new} in Eq. 9.1 using T_{new};
end
return T;

Algorithm 5: Hirechical FDA Guided Clustering (HFGC)

Input: X: samples
C: cluster labels of the samples
Output: C': updated labels
Initialize $C' = C$;
Calculate Fisher criterion J;
foreach *cluster c in unique*(C_i) **do**
  k-means clustering $\{x_i\}$ where $c_i = c$, $k = 2$;
  Update C' with new cluster labels;
  Calculate Fisher criterion J_{new};
  if $J_{new} < J$ **then**
    Revert back C';
  end
end
Return C';

9.3 Metric Learning

As discussed in Sect. 9.1, the feature vectors extracted from the same person in different cameras will be multi-modal, and LFDA will preserve such structure. Thus, a metric learning step is necessary to further compensate for the difference between two cameras.

Suppose z is the low-dimensional feature vector projected by the LFDA transformation matrix. Let the feature vector set for person p captured in camera a be $Z_p^a = \{z_1^a, z_2^a, \ldots, z_{n_p}^a\}$ where $z_i^a \in \mathbb{R}^m$. Then we take the sample mean of Z_p^a as the final descriptor for person p in camera a. Now the problem is reduced to the single-shot case, which can be solved using any metric learning technique. In our experiment, RankSVM [5, 6] is employed. The idea is to minimize the norm of a vector w which satisfies the following ranking relationship:

$$w^\top(|\bar{z}_i^a - \bar{z}_i^b| - |\bar{z}_i^a - \bar{z}_j^b|) > 0, \quad i, j = 1, 2, \ldots, P \ and \ i \neq j \tag{9.8}$$

where $\bar{z}_i^a$ is the sample mean feature vector of person i in camera a, and P is the total number of training subjects. The RankSVM method finds w by solving the problem

$$\begin{aligned} &\arg\min_{w,\xi}(\tfrac{1}{2}||w||^2 + C\sum_{i=1}^{P}\xi_i) \\ &s.t. \ w^\top(|\bar{z}_i^a - \bar{z}_i^b| - |\bar{z}_i^a - \bar{z}_j^b|) \geq 1 - \xi_i, \quad \xi_i \geq 0 \end{aligned} \tag{9.9}$$

where ξ_i is a slack variable.

9.4 Discussion

In this chapter, we are targeting specifically on multi-shot human re-identification problem, where instead of a single image, the probe is a sequence of images. How to gather information in an unbalance fashion is the key for a real-world re-identification problem. Here we proposed a unsupervised approach to extract the most representative key images from the probe sequence before learning the discriminative metric using LFDA algorithm.

References

1. R.A Fisher, The use of multiple measurements in taxonomic problems. Ann. Eugenics **7**(2), 179–188 (1936)
2. M. Sugiyama, Local fisher discriminant analysis for supervised dimensionality reduction, in *ACM International Conference on Machine Learning*, 2006

3. P. Niyogi, X. He, Locality preserving projections, in *Neural Information Processing Systems* (MIT, 2004)
4. Y. Li, Z. Wu, S. Karanam, R.J. Radke, Multi-shot human re-identification using adaptive Fisher discriminant analysis, in *British Machine Vision Conference*, 2015
5. B. Prosser, W.-S. Zheng, S. Gong, T. Xiang, Q. Mary, Person reidentification by support vector ranking, in *British Machine Vision Conference*, 2010
6. T. Joachims, Optimizing search engines using clickthrough data, in *ACM SIGKDD Conferences on Knowledge Discovery and Data Mining*, 2002

Chapter 10
Conclusions and Future Work

This chapter summarizes the work in this book and discuss ideas for future directions of research.

10.1 Summary

This book is a guide to practically developing a human re-identification system in real-world scenarios. The goal is to bridge the gap between academic research and industry, and discuss the practical challenges and their solutions in building a real-world human re-identification system.

The book begins with the introduction on the concept of intelligent video surveillance systems based on computer vision and machine-learning technologies. In particular, human re-identification is considered to be one of the most challenging problem in the domain of security surveillance, which shares certain overlapped approaches with traditional computer vision problems such as image retrieval and cross-view tracking. However human re-identification is a very targeted and specific application-oriented problem comes with certain limitations such as relatively lower image quality, requirement on scalability, as well as ranking-based evaluation pipeline.

In the second part of this book, we focused on the infrastructure design and planning of the human re-identification system. This is the part usually ignored by academic human re-identification researches. However we showed that the planning and design of the camera network, as well as accurate calibration of the intrinsic parameters of individual cameras and the extrinsic parameters of the camera network have very positive impact to the overall performance of the real-world re-identification system.

In the last part of the book, we focused on the specific problems related to the core analytics of the human re-identification problem. We addressed several main

Z. Wu, *Human Re-Identification*, Multimedia Systems and Applications,
DOI 10.1007/978-3-319-40991-7_10

problems that hinder human re-identification from being applied in real-world applications: first, perspective distortion and error from using the same descriptor to represent target images captured from different viewpoint angles. We proposed a sub-image rectification technique to eliminate perspective distortion from the camera viewpoint estimated by minimal calibration information. Then we introduced the concept of the pose prior, which can be learned offline and used to weight pixels at different spatial locations according to different viewpoint angles when generating feature descriptors. Third, we introduced an online learning approach to capture the discriminative for each individual online, to compensate the issue that the offline-learned metric heavily depending on the training data set. Then to cope with the fact that the dimensionality of most of the feature vectors used in human re-identification systems are very high and the training time is long, we proposed a framework combining random projection and random forest, to learn a discriminative metric while significantly reducing the signature dimension. Last but not least, an unsupervised image sequence key frame extraction approach is introduced, ensuring a balance sampling for multi-shot human re-identification.

The book is based on the author's experience accumulated in building a real-world human re-identification system in a major transportation environment, and has covered almost all aspects of practical issues one would encounter when trying to build a similar system. There is one most important lesson the author would like to share with the readers: always try to relate real-world scenarios to every aspect of the research problem you are working on, and think practically in designing every single step in your solution.

10.2 Future Work

Human re-identification is still a fairly new problem, and there are still quite a lot of open questions to be answered before we can really build a reliable and robust system and release human from the loop

10.2.1 Unified Benchmark Platform

Everyone tend to have his/her own evaluation protocol, which is very much a inefficiency for the community to evaluate and synchronize on the updates and progress of core analytic algorithms. While enforcing open-source may be difficult, it would be very useful to have a publicly available, unified benchmark platform, with which one can easily evaluate his/her algorithm with exactly the same configurations and setup as all baseline and state-of-the-art algorithms, on all available benchmark datasets.

10.2.2 *Modularized Pipeline*

A modularized pipeline design can be beneficial to real-world human re-identification. As we can see that there are five major relatively independent components for re-identification systems: tracking, preprocessing (e.g., rectification, enhancement, clustering, and association), feature extraction, metric learning, and matching. In order to have a generalized applicable system, every one of the above components needs to be interchangeable and adaptive. Modularized design together with a early fusion framework may be the right way to make a robust and stable real-world re-identification system.

10.2.3 *End-to-End Deep Neural Network for Human Re-Identification*

Deep learning has become popular in the community of computer vision, and many classical computer vision problem can now be learned end-to-end with deep learning, such as segmentation, detection and image search, etc. Deep learning approaches have been proposed for re-identification as well, including learning the representation by transfer learning. However we have not seen an end-to-end learned human re-identification system. The fundamental reason behind this is the lack of data. Deep learning approaches are data-hungry and the available benchmark dataset for human re-identification are all too small. A much larger dataset needs to be released to fully utilize the power of deep learning.

Index

Z. Wu, *Human Re-Identification*, Multimedia Systems and Applications,
DOI 10.1007/978-3-319-40991-7

Printed in the United States
By Bookmasters